SYSTEMOLOGY:

BACKTRACK

*Thank you for supporting independent publishing
and the Systemology Society.*

mardukite.com

MARDUKITE ACADEMY OF SYSTEMOLOGY PREMIERE EDITION

SYSTEMOLOGY:

BACKTRACK

RECLAIMING SPIRITUAL POWER AND PAST-LIFE MEMORY

Transcripts of the original lectures
by Joshua Free

Edited by Publications Officer, Addie Stone

THE JOSHUA FREE IMPRINT
JFI PUBLICATIONS

ISBN : 978-1-961509-13-9

Also available in hardcover.

A MARDUKITE SYSTEMOLOGY PUBLICATION
Mardukite Research Library Catalogue No. "Liber-4"
Developed for Mardukite Academy & Systemology Society

cum superiorum privilegio veniaque

FIRST EDITION PAPERBACK
August 2023

Published from
Joshua Free Imprint – JFI Publications
Mardukite Borsippa HQ, San Luis Valley, Colorado

Awaken to the New Dawn of Immortality!

We are all Spiritual Beings that have known a very long existence. Even before the evolution of Humans or Earth, we existed as other forms, in other times and spaces. We have descended down a very long *track* of potential Beingness and considerations, a *track* that parallels the allegory of "Fallen Angels" enticed by mundane bodies; only to be trapped in them and longing to *Ascend* again.

What if we could recover the long forgotten Knowingness of our past existences?

What if we could reclaim our true Spiritual power that we have lost sight of?

What if we could actually Backtrack our descent and return to the Source?

"Backtrack" documents the first advanced course given by Joshua Free to the Systemology Society for Grade-V. He candidly introduces the new Wizard-Level subject of Alpha-Defragmentation to Grade-III and Grade-IV alumni ready to embark on their next phase of the *Pathway.*

Now you too can learn to systematically process residual imprinting from "past-lives"—and not only expand your knowledge of "between-lives" spiritual implanting and other mental programming, but also how to handle it— exactly as experienced by advanced students attending a three-day lecture series at the Spring 2023 Conference at the Academy, commemorating the pre-release of the very first complete Beta-Defragmentation manual titled *"Systemology-180: The Fast-Track To Ascension."*

This premiere collector's edition hardcover publication of *"Systemology: Backtrack"* includes complete transcripts to *all eight lectures* along with a concise glossary for over 200 terms used in these lecture transcripts.

Free Your Spirit from the Human Track and Climb Aboard for a Flight Toward Ascension!

JOSHUA FREE'S
"THE BACKTRACK" LECTURE SERIES
MARCH 2023

∞

EDITOR'S NOTE

"The Self does not actualize Awareness
past a point not understood."
—*Tablets of Destiny*

This book contains transcripts from an advanced
lecture series given by Joshua Free to Grade-V
students of Mardukite Academy of Systemology in
March 2023 at the pre-release of "*Systemology-180.*"

Wherever a word that is defined in the glossary
first appears in these transcripts, it will be **bold**.

A clear understanding of this material is critical for
achieving actual realizations and personal benefit
from applying our philosophy as spiritual technology.

The *Seeker* should be especially certain not to simply
"read through" this book without attaining proper
comprehension as "knowledge." Even when the
information continues to be "interesting"—if at any
point you find yourself feeling lost or confused while
reading, trace your steps back. Return to the point of
misunderstanding and go through it again.

Take nothing within this book on faith.
Apply the information directly to your life.

Decide for yourself.

∞

Transcripts for the Lecture Series
given to the Systemology Society
in March 2023, originally titled:
Reclaiming Your Spiritual Power by
Systematically Processing Past-Lives

MARDUKITE GRADE-V, WIZARD LEVEL-1 SYSTEMOLOGY SUMMARY & OVERVIEW[*] "THE NEW DAWN OF IMMORTALITY"

Greetings *Seekers*—

Welcome to Systemology Grade-V!

Let us take a moment here to catch up and get on the same page before delving further along the *Pathway*.

Many **Seekers** crossing paths with our Systemology actually do so by routes of "magic" and "mysticism"—and what is *magic* really, but an attempted **codification** of *mysticism.* "**Religion**" is, of course, yet another way in which to make efforts to understand *spiritual systems.* But here in this physical universe, here on planet Earth at the very least, these *routes* have only offered glimpses and hints to what is otherwise never understood perfectly. And whenever truths are actually gleaned, they are done so through an individual's own filters of understanding—seeming to be very real for themselves, who are in agreement with it—but it is never even perfectly communicated thereafter. The perfect duplication of an "originating" experience is never really able to be passed to another—and even if it were, that other individual would still perceive it within the confines of their own filters of understanding. In essence, this mode has led us to a **system** or Universe comprised of **agreements** from the 'lowest common denominator' so to speak.

When we consider *magic* as a "codified" or "**systematized**" understanding of *mysticism,* or what is otherwise *spiritual* phenomenon, what we are really seeing is a progressive or **gradient** course of breaking agreements with the Physical Universe—to rise above the **imprints** and **implants** that fix our **attention** and **considerations** to

---

[*]   This introduction was first issued as a printed hand-out to attendees of the Grade-V *"Backtrack"* Lectures by Joshua Free in March 2023.

the low-**level** "**reality**" of this *Beta-Existence.* This is the *Great Work,* in effect, what **esoteric** circle have whispered of for thousands of years concerning a "Great Magical Arcanum"—an incommunicable understanding, an **awareness** of **realization**, that all of the facets have pointed to collectively but which is never generally found from any one avenue of pursuit exclusively. Nor does an individual benefit from perpetually spinning the dial on an intellectual combination lock with the hope that they will randomly and miraculously crack the safe and open the vault cover to the perfected true **knowledge** and supreme understanding.

The present author's development of "Systemology" resulted from a quarter-of-a-century dedicated to "practical occultism" and "esoteric avenues" of exploration and experimentation in the 'New Age' underground. In all that time, dozens of literary discourses (books) were given on those subjects directly, chronicling the *Pathway* taken specifically by the present author. Is this the only way in which answers could be gleaned? Perhaps not. But such an outline *was* refined and presented along the way—and when completed, when a bird's eye overview was finally accessible, it revealed a strong parallel to the *actual* "Gates" separating this Universe (and its participants) from the ALL. Consequently, in 2019, the "Grades" (now used to represent the "Mardukite Academy") were distinguished—not only for intellectual purposes, but specifically to define very tangible and finite *gradients* or *ledges* of actualized realizations and increased Awareness; what some individuals might classify as *states* of Beingness.

THE GRADES OF MARDUKITE ACADEMY

Systemology begins with Grade-III, partly based on earlier research developments. Pursuits into the theory and practical **methodology** of "Systemology" occurred consecutive with the original work of the Mardukite Chamberlains (*Mardukite Org.*) starting as early as 2008. Of course, the actual emphasis at the time is what we now consider "Grade-II" for our system. Our complete educational system is presently as follows (defined for the "Mardukite Academy"):

Grade-I   Route of Mysticism (and Magic)
Grade-II   Route of Mardukite Mesopotamia (Religion)
Grade-III Mardukite Systemology [Master Level]
Grade-IV   Metahuman Systemology [Wizard Lvl-0]
Grade-V   Metaspiritual Systemology [Wizard Lvl-1]

SYSTEMOLOGY TECHNIQUES

The "systematic **processing**" techniques for what is now "Class-1 Piloting" originally developed as an advanced methodology for "Mardukite Ministers" to practice spiritual advisement and religious counseling from within our unique tradition. This is, perhaps, most evident in the primary "Class-1" textbook, "*The Tablets of Destiny (Revelation)*" [*Liber-One*]. Unquestionably, it paved the way for solid developments of "Grade-III" work (and above) in an innovative, new and relevant way not elsewhere explored in the commercial 'New Age' or even the 'esoteric underground'. Additionally, as relayed in "*The Power of Zu*" lectures, increased urgency on its behind-the-scenes development resulted from efforts toward personal rehabilitation following an incident in October 2015, when the present author was struck by a large truck while walking. Were it not for our Systemology, there would have been no additional work by Joshua Free from then onward. This is not stated to give some 'wild' testimonial to our work; but the facts remain as they are.

A complete collection of "Grade-III" work developed for nearly a decade behind-the-scenes before its back-to-back release in late 2019. By the end of 2021, the Systemology Society completed an additional **tier** of developments—"Grade-IV"—which ended with a proverbial '*Wall of Fire*' that we must now cross in order to achieve any higher vistas with additional *Grades*. But certainly, no one actively involved or **participating** in this program can dispute the positive gains and tremendous accomplishments demonstrated by the solid work performed thus far—a collection of knowledge and techniques that we are now able to reflect on in its entirety with the new Grade-V volume, "<u>Systemology-180: The Ascension Manual (A Handbook for Pilots)</u>."

PILOTING AND PROCESSING

There are two coinciding "lanes" of the *Pathway* leading toward the same basic gradients (or "states" if you prefer): *Piloting* and *Processing*. The first is traveled primarily by "training" (particularly from books and lectures) with supplemental applications of "systematic processing"; whereas the second is accomplished by an untrained *Seeker* that is "processed" with the guidance and direction of a trained *Pilot*. A *Seeker* working alone has only the first option—to be their own *Solo Pilot*. As such, they are responsible for all the training as a *Pilot* and also the processing as a *Seeker*. Determination must be high in order to successfully "Fly Solo" since there is no one else to help maintain a *Seeker's* **"presence"** in "session" or to keep them from "free-spinning" in thought if they stray from a technique.

"Flying Solo" for the entire *Pathway* may require a longer more intensive journey, but it can still yield stable results. There is, however, a common misconception among our readers, that books and training for *Pilots* only apply to **processing** *others*. This is most certainly not the case. *Piloting* is the proper handling of "systematic processing" whether it is applied alone to *Self* or applied to *Self* under the direction of someone else. In either case, to be effective, the same systematic knowledge must be applied; it must be *Piloted*—even when the *Pilot* and *Seeker* are the same individual.

Whether a *Seeker* is operating alone or not, all techniques of "systematic processing" are *Self-processed*; they all must be processed by *Self*. A *Pilot* is only directing attention, but the "command lines" are not a magic spell delivered by a magic wand. The *Pilot* is not "doing" anything *to* the *Seeker*; the *Seeker* must apply the "command lines" of the technique to *Self* as *Self*. This systematic application of **communication** and **intention** is what makes "processing" possible or effective. It is the same principle that allows all other metaphysical and spiritual techniques any effectiveness; however, our Systemology Grades simply employ the most direct applications of the underlying fundamentals that yield significant results without a lot of excessive mystical or religious themes draped on top unnecessarily.

GRADE PROCESSING AND PILOT CLASSIFICATIONS

The basic gradients and presently existing classifications —as well as our publications representing them for the "Mardukite Academy"—are:

—*Grade-III*—

Class-1   Systemology: The Original Thesis [*Liber-S1X*]
          "The Power of Zu" Lecture Series [*Liber-S1Z*]
          Tablets of Destiny (Revelation) [*Liber-One*]
Class-2* Crystal Clear: Handbook for Seekers [*Liber-2B*]
          "Mardukite Systemology" Academy Lectures‡

---

* Each *Class* is a prerequisite for a "higher" *Class*. The material subsequently builds upon itself to form a greater and more complete understanding of the "big picture" being communicated overall.

‡ Available in "*The Complete Mardukite Master Course*" (anthology) and "*Mardukite Systemology: Mardukite Master Course Academy Lectures (Volume 4).*"

—Grade-IV—

Class-2C	Metahuman Destinations [*Liber-2C,2D,3C*][†]
Class-3	Imaginomicon [*Liber-3D*]
Class-3E	The Way of the Wizard [*Liber-3E*]

Each systematic processing "Route" along the *Pathway* **correlates** to specific technical documents (or "flight manuals") containing basic information and instructions for a *Pilot* to operate specific techniques toward a finite result or **end-point**. "Route-1" and "Route-2" are described in Grade-III; while "Route-3" and "Route-0" pertain to Grade-IV. The complete training is contained within half-a-dozen books that introduce the theory and practice of various exercises. The actual techniques themselves are now collected in the upper-level reference volume, "<u>*Systemology-180: The Fast-Track to Ascension (A Handbook for Pilots)*</u>," which is primarily of high-power value to those individuals that have completed the full Grade-III and Grade-IV education on its proper application to "systematic processing" and everyday life.

PERSONAL DEFRAGMENTATION

The emphasis and goal of the portion of the *Pathway* given above is a preliminary to "**Ascension**," a stable point of elevated realization and Awareness, which we define as "**Beta-Defragmentation**." —And by "*Beta*" we, of course, mean *this* Physical Universe; and where it applies to the *Human Condition* (in Grade-III and Grade-IV), we mean *this* present 'incarnation' or **association** of an 'Identity' with a specific physical meat-body life-cycle of a '*genetic vehicle*'. As it is comprised of all Grade-III and Grade-IV material, "Class-3E" training is the only level of completion that covers enough detail to ensure a total "Beta-Defragmentation" regimen properly.

---

† Reissued as two volumes in 2022.

> The **Alpha-Spirit** has one singular continuous life-track or **'Spiritual Timeline'** that is experienced in *Beta-Existence* as the separate life-times of a *'Genetic Vehicle'* or some other *body.*

"Defragmentation" is the personal processing of the **conditions** and upsets that impinge on an individual's ability, attention and/or Awareness to fully Self-determine and Self-direct a high quality of experience (**existence**). In Grade-III and Grade-IV, the emphasis of 'systematic processing' remains on what is most accessible to an individual regarding experience during *this* "life"—but as we have discovered, much of the incidental imprinting taking place during *this* "lifetime" is really only detrimental because it is compounded onto a long "string" or "chain" of earlier similar and comparatively more significant imprints (and implants) on the **Backtrack.** And this is where we inevitably run up against what many refer to as *"past-lives."*

EXPLORING THE BACKTRACK (PAST-LIVES)

The *"Spiritual Timeline"* is a primary focus and emphasis of the higher level "Wizard Grades" in our Systemology—and when referring to that part of the **timeline** which is 'past', we began to refer to it as the *"Backtrack"*—and thus the first new core volume of our Grade-V material will be concisely titled: *"Systemology: Backtrack."*

"Past-Lives" are only **semantically** described as such from the perspective of the birth-growth-death-cycle inherent in the incarnation of a physical body, that we refer to as a *'Genetic Vehicle'*, because it is independent of the actual *Self*, though an individual (*Alpha-Spirit*) may certainly be **fragmented** enough to wholly *consider* "itself" *as* the physical body in totality. This mentality is what prompts the desires for material greed or the 'fight' for survival in a physical universe, when in actuality, the

Alpha-Spirit, the actual *Awareness* of *Self*, is "eternal" and cannot help but to go on "spiritually" existing and surviving. When a 'genetic vehicle' "dies" the *Alpha-Spirit* most certainly goes on to "live another day" as another form. Virtually every religion and spiritual philosophy suggests so, though the general understanding of this is not based in truths and therefore not carried with certainty by folk in their everyday life on Earth.

Our interest in the *Backtrack* is unique to our Systemology. Although for thousands of years, "past-lives" are frequently the subject of discussion in theosophical and metaphysical circles, there has been little codification or systematic understanding associated with it. For example, our interests are primarily on the "spiritual timeline" of the *Alpha-Spirit*. Such data is too often confused with the *cellular* or **genetic memory** of the physical organism 'used' by an *Alpha-Spirit*. "Genetic memory" *can* affect the Human experience—and operation of a 'genetic vehicle'—but the implications are only as significant as the *Alpha-Spirit* considers themselves to be 'Identified' *as* that 'genetic vehicle' (and no longer themselves as an 'Individual'). The *Self* takes on that "record" when it confuses the "I" with the "my" (in regards to a "body" as a separate entity). And of course, when the "body" is injured or **pinged**, the **sensation** forces attention and *Awareness* of the *Alpha-Spirit* to "snap-in" on the "body."

SPIRITUAL TECHNOLOGY OF ASCENSION

On the surface, there are very few practical differences between the technical theory behind "Beta-Defragmentation" and what we consider "**Alpha**-Defragmentation" techniques (or else the proverbial "A.T." work we have been pursuing at the Systemology Society for many years). For the most part, only the consideration of significance and importance differs in regards to where 'systematic processing' is directed—and, of course, the associated *Pilot* training necessary to systematically handle the *Backtrack*. In some cases, it is also quite possible that imprinting and implanting from the *Backtrack* could effectively 'stall' or **inhibit** successful Beta-Defragmentation if it is actively triggered or in stimulation. This, of course, must be handled—which means a *Pilot* must be prepared to do so. We are not directly exploring "past-lives" in Grade-III and Grade-IV, but should such data emerge during these early processes, the matter cannot be ignored. Such training falls under the classification of Grade-V, and again, that proverbial "A.T." work.

DEFINING THE ADVANCED "A.T." SYSTEMOLOGY WORK

Much of Grade-IV (such as "*Imaginomicon*") is considered "pre-A.T." work, also called Wizard Level-0; whereas Grade-V is the first true "A.T." gradient, and Wizard Level-1. The term "A.T." came about during semantic debates concerning how to precisely categorize the "Wizard-Level" work of our Systemology. But, in the end, the basic list seemed to surround the same general ideas—and fortunately, the same alphabetic letters:

—A—	—T—
Alpha	*Techniques*
Actualization	*Technology*
Ascension	*Technician*
Advanced	*Training*

"Years ago, we realized that 'The Way Out' would systematically resemble the routes by which we descended. We understood that the 'Gates' reflected in our most archaic esoteric lore were pointing toward a *realization* that had been lost in translation along the way— and that our only hope of finding a *Map* to this *Pathway* was in recovering that lost under- standing. I believe that our Systemology is successfully delivering a communication that is unparalleled into today's society, and most of you can attest that above and beyond the former gradients of knowledge available to us in our world, this work we are doing now is our best chance at 'making the grade' to reach our *Ascension* in *this* lifetime—and for the first time in a very long time, reclaim the true power of the *Alpha-Spirit* and the freedom to experience an existence of our own true *Self- determined* creation. "

—*Joshua Free*

THE SYSTEMOLOGY

BACKTRACK

LECTURE SERIES

ORGANIC EVOLUTION -VS.- SPIRITUAL TIMELINE (BACKTRACK)

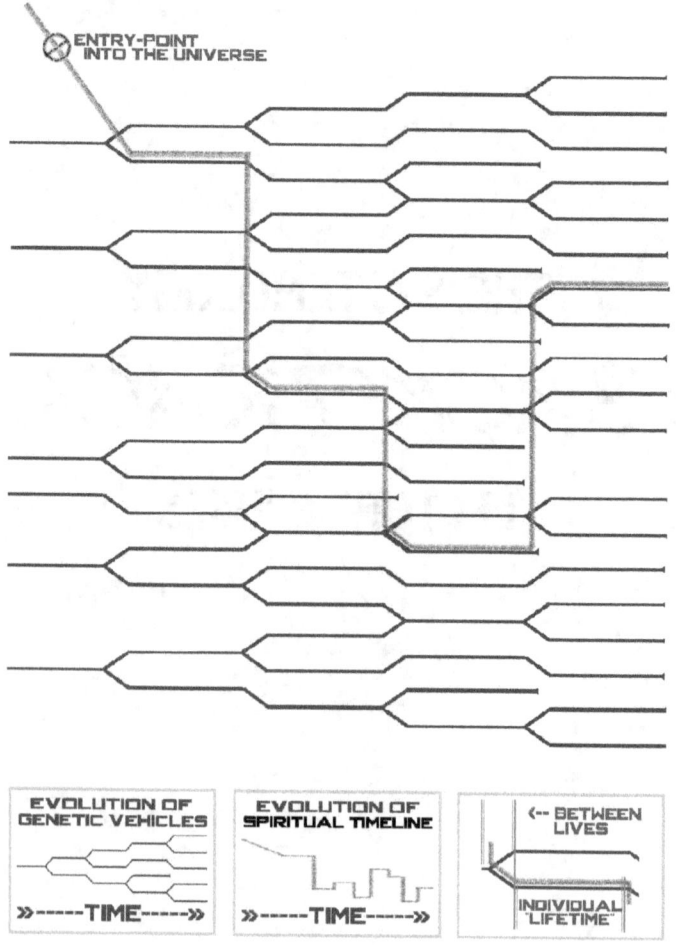

A representative example for demonstration use only.

.: LECTURE ONE :.
INTRODUCING THE BACKTRACK
17, MARCH 2023

Greetings, *Seekers*—and welcome to the *Mardukite Academy of Systemology* "Grade-V" Spring 2023 Lecture Series. Now, in Grade-V Systemology ("*Wizard Level-1*"), we are primarily concerned with recovery of spiritual power—which is to say, our *Actualized* **Awareness**—from the "*Backtrack.*" This subject has remained of great interest to our **Seekers** for many years. However, it begins to open up areas of "*Alpha-Defragmentation*"—a **gradient** above the *Beta-Defragmentation* handled in Grade-III and Grade-IV—and therefore is classified as "Wizard-Level" work. And while it has admittedly taken a few years to reach this stable ledge, here we are.

When we refer to the "Backtrack" in Systemology, we mean specifically that which is *past*. Technically, any use of "recall" in systematic **processing** pertains to the "Backtrack"—however, when we speak of it in our work, it generally indicates what most **individuals** understand as "past-lives." And this is a subject that is above the tolerance **level** or acceptance-**band** of communication and understanding among **standard-issue** "Humans" in modern society. It has even been pointed out to me that in the millions of words I've written and/or presented on esoteric, mystical or systemological subjects in the past 27 years, very little (if anything) has been stated directly by me on the subject of "past-lives" or "reincarnation"— and this is no accident.

There *are* references to the "Backtrack" all throughout previous publications on Systemology—though they generally are accompanied by suggestions that we would be **treating** it more directly at the higher Wizard-Levels. That being said: I'm opening this lecture series officially as "*Class-4*"—which, of course, means there is a certain expectancy to the background of a *Seeker* wanting to apply it to processing and for personal growth. The basics of our *applied philosophy* are covered elsewhere, in earlier courses. And as a portable assistant or reference volume for our Wizard-Level work, all of the former "Routes" and techniques of *Grade-III* and *Grade-IV* have now been concisely revised and collected for the new release: "*Systemology-180: The Fast Track to Ascension*" (*Liber-180*).

While it does not replace knowing a lot of the general background information on Systemology, "*Liber-180*" does replace having to fan through hundreds of pages among several books when looking for just the practical instructions or when compiling the full selection of exercises necessary for a complete *Beta-Defragmentation* regimen. We've now done that work for you. But the proper handling of that information is critical for higher-level success. Some of the techniques there only require minor modifications to effectively apply to the "Backtrack."

The first *Grade-V* alteration to our standard **methodology** is that we are no longer restricting our attention to the **incarnation** of a 'genetic vehicle' in *this* "lifetime." This was never really a "hard rule" in earlier Grades. But, I had good reasons for holding off on a "Backtrack" emphasis until now. These reasons will be more obviously **apparent** as we trek through this course.

In *Mardukite Systemology Grade-V*—designated "Spiritual Systemology" or "Metaspiritual Systemology"—we are treating the "Backtrack" as "*Route-4*." Thus, we have a bit of consistency in classifying "Class-4" **Piloting** with "Route-4" Tech treated materially in published form as the "*Liber-4*" series. So, anywhere you now find the *four* represented in our material, you know that it pertains to the "Backtrack." And this includes anything in the "4-series"—such as "*Route-4G*" pertaining to using a **GSR-Meter** for systematic processing, and so forth, since you know we often append "letters" to our numeric sequencing. We also just so happen to be in our fourth active year of Systemology, since we brought it public in 2019 with the publication of *"The **Tablets of Destiny**" (**Liber-One**)*, after almost a decade of underground behind-the- scenes development.

The numbers designating the processing and training "Routes" may seem arbitrary—and most *Grade-IV Seekers* are not even aware of their original significance. This is because it was never addressed directly in the texts. Prior to the establishment of the "Mardukite Academy" in 2020, our 2019 research staff **participated** in developing the *"**Beta-Awareness Test**" (**BAT**)* found in *"**Crystal Clear**"* (and reprinted in *"The Way Into The Future"* and original *"Systemology Handbook"*), which was also integral to our *"Beta-Awareness Scale"* as described in the same text(s), and of course related to our principle *"**Standard Model**."* All of this data was taken into consideration when plotting out our standard "Routes" of systematic processing.

In late 2019, the first two processing methods—"**Route-1**" and "**Route-2**"—were targeting specific levels of *Beta-Awareness.* The goal of *Beta-Defragmentation* is always to increase a *Seeker's* "actual" *Awareness,* no matter what Route is taken. It was assumed, and has since been established, that an individual could only be processed or communicated with in certain ways depending on their present level of *Actualized Awareness* at a given time. This is true just about always, everywhere, but became more visibly obvious and critical in our Systemology work. As a result, "Route-1" was originally intended to handle a *Seeker* hovering around "1" on the *Beta-Awareness Scale;* with "Route-2" serving better for those hovering around "2" and so forth.

Some of this should be a common understanding to an experienced *Pilot*—or an application of mild intuition. You've got a guy that's just been hit by a car, and he's hovering around lower than "1" and just in real bad shape. The thing to do is *not* start asking him to recall a **time** he was in good communication with his mom or something. You've got to deal with what is pressing hard against the *Seeker* in present time and impinging on their attentions and *Awareness*. Without this, you've got no "**presence**" in session. The guy's not "there"; there's no *Seeker* to process. You take what is available and increase it. And you use the right tool for the right job.

Of course, the "Routes" do not *only* apply to specific *Beta-Awareness* levels; but it serves to establish a sort of minimum criteria for the level of processing and education that falls *within* an individual's tolerance band of acceptance—what they actually have a **reality** on or a **willingness** to **confront**. In *"The Complete Mardukite Master Course"* we speak often of "entry points" concerning the instruction of a student, but the same principle applies to our general handling of Systemology. The progressive effectiveness of the Pathway to elevate *Awareness* is also **proportional** to the *Actualized Awareness* applied at each gradient. So, the development must be systematically balanced to be both stable *and* continue moving upward.

A *Seeker* that has no reality on recalling significant *facets* from yesterday, or *analytically processing* an incident from childhood, is going to be running up against a lot of obstacles, if they are suddenly forced to confront a '*Spiritual Timeline*' involving "Shared Universes" going back four-quadrillion years, **relatively** speaking. Of course, a person does not have to be scoring a solid "4.0" on a *Beta-Awareness Test* in order to use "Route-4." But, a *Seeker* must be approached from a stable ledge, using solid gradients of realization, that they can reach from. And that's what we are doing all along the way, systematically.

We have not *avoided* the "Backtrack" in former work, but it has not been an emphasis. It would be impossible to *avoid* altogether, given how advanced our spiritual philosophy is in Systemology. And the keyword there is: "*spir-itual.*" We are, after all, dealing with the *Alpha-Spirit*. The *Alpha-Spirit* is the actual *Self*, the I-AM, back of all that has been considered. It is the one doing the considering—the one doing the looking. It is *you*. It is *me*. And we have been traveling down a *long* track to arrive here now, and with such close attachment to the **Human Condition**.

The *Spirit* can *consider* that it has had many **experiences** with many incarnated *bodies*, but the *Spirit* itself has but *one* spiritual life—for it *is* Spiritual Life. It may have fixed its own *Awareness* to countless forms and **existences** and incidents along the way. But still, we are dealing with *one* continuous '*spiritual* **continuum**' for each of us. We are dealing with the same **ZU-line** this entire time—the same "Standard Model" all the way. Only our level of under-standing has changed as we moved up into these higher gradients; and boy has it changed!

There is another critical point I must address before we move into this work much further. It has come to my at-tention that over the past few years, many *Seekers* have shied away from the "Pilot-oriented" manuals and les-sons, thinking that the material only applies to systemat-ic processing of *others.* This is a false assumption. When I asked someone why they hadn't looked in "**Metahuman Destinations**" yet, they responded, like: "Oh, isn't that a *Piloting* course? I'm working alone on this stuff and trying to get a handle on it before I apply it to someone else." Oh, boy. That's exactly the type of individual that *needs* the books as course material, especially lacking the direct contact with others.

Piloting is the name given to the handler of systematic processing in our tradition. Whether someone is *Co-Pilot-ing* someone else, or "Flying Solo" by themselves, if sys-tematic processing is involved, it must be *Piloted*. This means following all the guidelines gleaned from former "Routes" to a systematic processing *session*. I mean—

would you only learn how to fly a plane if it involved carrying passengers? Shouldn't a *Pilot* have an expert handling of their technology when alone? This is important to consider as you explore the upper-level work and publications.

There is simply no substitute for understanding the Systemology developments that have carried us up to these higher gradients, particularly if an individual intends to get as much out of this work as possible, in terms of stable **realizations.** And to understand the "Backtrack" requires an understanding of what it consists of—a basic understanding of the fundamental principles behind our entire Systemology. This means: the *Alpha-Spirit*, which has been the focus of our work since the beginning; and also the "Standard Model" and *ZU-line*, on which our entire applied philosophy was based. Since this has been covered extensively elsewhere, let us turn our attention then to the main subject at hand for Grade-V.

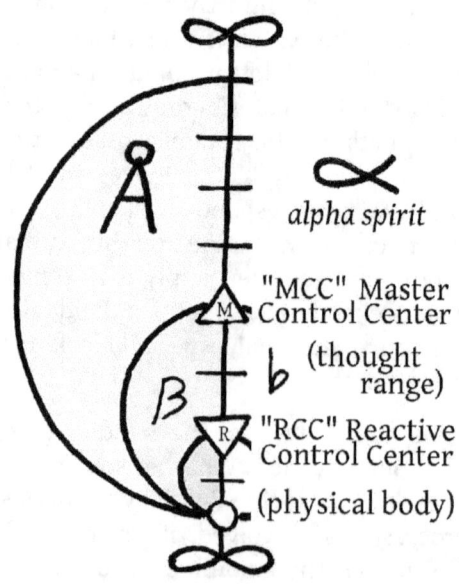

alpha spirit

"MCC" Master Control Center

(thought range)

"RCC" Reactive Control Center

(physical body)

For eons the state of the Human Condition has reflected being lost in a **fragmented** haze—or the darkness of confusion. And while there have been a few "beacons of light" along the way, most of these degraded into little more than a slight illumination of the pervading darkness. Still, a *Seeker* was left with no clear map *out* from these **conditions**, which are made to appear as though they surround *Self* in all directions. My dedication to charting such a *map* is not an attempt to offer "*hope*," but to offer *answers* and a means toward personal certainty.

It is not my goal to revise thousands of years of religious beliefs point-for-point. Some of what is discovered within our Spiritual Systemology will certainly validate some key areas that pertain to **religions** spanning across history. Of course, there are also some unique aspects of our work that will not be altogether synchronous with what may be considered "standard" among the present masses. We are not in the business of convincing humanity of anything specifically. Our Systemology has always worked with what produces effective results towards our specific goals at each step, regardless of where the information came from or what preexisting understanding others may have formerly carried about it.

In combination with decades of exploration into various mystical, spiritual and otherwise **esoteric** avenues, my vision for Systemology since the mid-1990's has been to present it as an evolution of a uniquely American-styled tradition called "The New Thought." At its **inception**, "New Thought" was the American transcendentalist answer to the European "magickal revival" taking place at the end of the 19th century. Unfortunately, over the past century, "New Thought" degraded into more commercial 'New Age' *puffery*. But, one of the most prolific original pioneers of "The New Thought" movement, William Walker Atkinson, probably inspired and more significantly influenced my earliest systemological endeavors than any others in the genre. He quite eloquently describes the fragmented experience typical in one's lifetime, for those with enough *Actualized Awareness* to recognize that there is something *more* than *Beta-Existence*:

"We are like the squirrel in the cage, who exhausts himself in traveling the long road of the wheel, only to find himself, at the end of his journey, just where he started. Or worse still, like the newly-caged wild bird, we dash ourselves against the bars of our mental prison, again and again, in our efforts to gain freedom, until at last we lie weak and bleeding, a captive still.

"We have sought to climb the Mountain of **Knowledge**, urged on by the thought of the place of blissful rest at the summit. We have toiled wearily up the steep and stony sides, and finally with bleeding hands and tired feet—with body and mind exhausted by our efforts—we reach the summit and congratulate ourselves upon the ending of our task. But when we look around us, lo! Our mountain is but a foothill. Far above us, towering higher and higher, rise range after range of the real mountains, the highest peaks being hidden among the clouds.

"We have felt that hunger for Spiritual Knowledge that transcended the hunger for bread. We have sought this way and that way for the 'Bread of Life'—and found it not. We have asked this **authority** and that authority for the 'Bread' that would nourish the 'Spirit', but we were given nothing but the 'stone' of **'dogma'** and creeds. At last, we sank exhausted, and felt there was no 'Bread' to be had —that it was all a delusion, a will-o'-the-wisp of the mind—that there was no reality to it.

"But we forgot, that just as the hunger of the body implies that somewhere in the world is to be found that which will satisfy it—that just as the hunger of the mind implies that somewhere is to be found mental nourishment—so the mere fact that this spiritual hunger exists, is a sure indication that somewhere there exists that which the Absolute has intended to satisfy it. The hunger implies a **potential** for fulfillment. The trouble is that we have been seeking outside that which we can only find within. The Kingdom of Heaven is within you."

Prior to our Systemology, mainstream religions and popular esoteric interpretations circulating underground may have offered glimpses and potential at reversing movement on a downward track, but the results—the present state of the Human Condition—speaks for itself. The spiritual health and wellbeing—the *Actualized Awareness*—of our fellow "citizen" is evident. The visible route and direction that the whole thing is headed is unmistakable. Of course, you have to be actually *looking* in order to see it; and we know from experimental experience in Systemology that there are many individuals that cannot even provide a *presence* enough to properly *confront* the room in which they have the body seated, let alone the greater environment out there that they are told is dangerous to actually *look* at—and which they can then take no **responsibility** for and therefore have no power to change anything about it. But that isn't even the *game* we are playing at directly. We are simply clearing the lens in order to improve an individual's ability to *look*; we are not arbitrating what they choose to *look at*.

To handle the "Backtrack"—or to even have a better understanding of any experience in life—it is important to understand *who* is doing the actual *looking*. The "**Route-0**" (and "**3D**") techniques and "Wizard Level-0" meditations are intended to give a *Seeker* a greater certainty on *Self* as the *Alpha-Spirit*, and not as a **personality**-package; to establish the spiritual essence of *Beingness* as an *Aware-*

ness and not clinging to some artificial "**Identity**." This may all seem like *just* "words" until their **semantics**—their meaning—is actually realized and understood by personal demonstration, even if only subjectively. Such exercises are mostly found in "*Imaginomicon*" (**Liber-3D**) and reprinted in "*The Metahuman Systemology Handbook*" anthology—and, of course, summarized in "*Systemology-180.*"

The subject of the "Backtrack" involves the same **premise** that our entire Systemology is rooted from—the same main subject introduced on the first lines of my "*Original Thesis*" over a decade ago—and that is the *Alpha-Spirit*. And I had to develop a rudimentary vocabulary to distinguish the specific understanding I wanted relayed in Systemology, because former semantics and meanings as people generally know them didn't seem applicable. This was true of religion and metaphysics. Therefore, I chose the term *Alpha-Spirit* to represent a new and better understanding of what is otherwise misunderstood by any other name. So, I avoided this word "soul" that seemed wrapped in too many religious connotations already anyways. For example, I found myself to be quite in agreement with Atkinson, when he explains that the actual *Self* or I-AM *is* what people call the "soul"—and that it is not something *separate* from *Self*; that it is not something you *have*. And this scares a lot of low-Aware-ness individuals because they have other semantic attachments to this idea and all they hear me say is "you don't *have* a soul." But, a few other obscure sects have caught on to this as well. Anyways, he says:

> "To many who believe that they will live beyond the grave, it seems as if something which they call 'my soul' will arise from the ruins of their body and will go on to live forever.

> "To those in whom spiritual **consciousness** has already been awakened, a different **concept** pres-

ents itself. They feel the I-AM consciousness strong within them, and know that, no matter what may happen to the body, the 'Real Self' will live on.

"They know that that which they call 'I' *is* the soul, and are not deceived by the thought that the soul is something that is going to put in an appearance after the 'I' lies down in death. There is every difference between the two concepts. The whole question hinges on this distinction. The 'soul' is not a thing apart from yourself—it is *you*—you *are* the soul."

Anything that the *Alpha-Spirit* carries with it along the '*Spiritual Continuum*' is a product or creation of its own **considerations**—however much these might also have been coerced, **enforced** or **implanted** along the way. Near the completion of an effectively run *Beta-Defragmentation* regimen, a *Seeker* arrives at the realization that the *Alpha-Spirit*—the I-AM, the *Self*—is actually *non-local*. It may have fixed its '**point-of-view**' to a singular locatable **viewpoint**. But, its true *Beingness* is not located in the time-**space** of *this*, or any, *Beta-Existence*. It has not actually left from its original '**static**' position as a '*Spiritual Unit*' of *Awareness*. It has, however, manifested many **postulates**, taken on many layers of consideration and, of course, '*reality-**agreements**' to communicate in '*Shared-Universes*' with others. It may even be on a downward spiral of compounded and **condensed** postulates and considerations for its own *Beingness*—but one thing we can be sure of is that an *eternal spirit* goes on being *eternal.* Atkinson's words continue:

"It is *you* who lives on forever, not some intangible thing that develops from you at the hour of death. This *you* is living in Eternity as much now as it ever will be. *This* is Eternity—right *now*. Many of us, before we grow into an understanding of things, feel that this life is of no consequence—that it is a mis-

erable thing and that true living will not begin until we get out of the body and become a 'Spirit'. You
are a Spirit as much now as ever."

There are a few other unique aspects of our "Backtrack"
Systemology that should be pointed out here at the start,
because they often times collide with more fanciful
thinking found in traditional religions, the contemporary
'New Age', and even many forms of mysticism. Such aspects don't especially bode well for popularity contests,
but I've always attested to desiring to be right rather
than popular any day. I can understand why certain spiritual lessons might have been communicated as they
were in the past; but we have already traversed the last
6,000 years of written and recorded teachings at the Mardukite Academy in Grade-I and Grade-II, and soon after
discovered there was a lot more ground to be tread on
the Pathway to Ascension.

So, we certainly acknowledge the existence of an eternal
Alpha-Spirit and that there is a Pathway of Ascension. In
Grade-IV, we could also attest to the realization that at
the core, the Alpha-Spirit has near-infinite capabilities for
postulating, creating, considering and so forth—which,
when left unchecked, has led to a **successive** series of
condensing reality-agreements and Universes in which
to occupy our point-of-view. These veils of separation
represent a progressive "fall" from our true and natural
or basic spiritual state. And some of this is reflected in
between the lines of many spiritual teachings of the ages;
but then why do they assume that the inherent course
direction being followed by humanity should inevitably
lead back to these higher states? Why do they speak of
the "soul's evolution" as if it were something that is automatically reached—and speak of it as though it were
some newly discovered destination that we had not
already descended from previously?

Either the spiritual mystic was once misled, or they went on to mislead others, following behavior **patterns** dictated by one or another implant. Or, perhaps they were simply mistaken by assuming that since they, themselves, had taken up their own understanding of the *Pathway*—they were already operating in a higher state of "spiritual consciousness" or *Actualized Awareness* than the standard-issue Human—then they may have assumed that eventually all others would thereafter follow. But, a *Self-Honest* approach to the "Backtrack" has revealed that this is not the case—that the "natural" progression of things as they are, is not "upward." This is what our Systemology seeks to correct—and why our present focus refers so much to what is "past" or doing a turn-around or 180-**degree** 'about-face' on the course the standard-issue Human Condition (and, of course, the *Alpha-Spirit* entrapped to considerations of the same) is currently following.

This is perhaps, one of the key areas that split my work from those that inspired my original endeavors. Because, while I have to assume Atkinson had caught on to this fact, it is not what he communicated to the early supporters of "The New Thought" movement at the beginning of the 20th century. The issue behind this is that while most of the basic tenets of the teachings are well-grounded, this flavor of "The New Thought" later evolved into the more *fluffy* and commercialized or popular aspects of spiritualism associated with the 'New Age' today. They are "popular" and more "marketable" because there are some spiritual ideals that some folks would simply *prefer* to believe, rather than to quest for, **discern** and realize an **undefiled** *Self-Honest* truth for themselves.

Another critical assumption that Systemology dispels is this idea that one naturally elevates to a higher level of enlightenment or automatically reaches a true *Ascension* simply because the 'genetic vehicle' dies. I mean—sure, you've just *dropped* a body; but chances are pretty good that without some kind of proactive work along the *Pathway*, the individual is not going out of this lifetime free of the ensnared or entrapped considerations that have been taken on. This is what we mean by "***process-out***": that an individual is releasing their hold on something **compulsively** created, even if unknowingly, that *is* an energetic "mass" on, let us say, a "thought-level"; and therefore represents the kind of spiritual "baggage" or "contamination" that is *weighing* the *Alpha-Spirit* down to low-level considerations of *Beingness* and *Existence*.

The **allegory** of "fallen angels"—beings that were once high in their actualized existence, ensnared by the desire for **sensation** and entrapped within considerations of material bodies, is essentially the story of us all. The exact details are certainly more involved than the bedtime-story versions surviving in contemporary religious literature, but the sentiment is similar—and the example is valid for our purposes.

Even when confined to considerations of this *Beta-Existence*, there is obviously a "between-lives" period where the *Alpha-Spirit* is not burdened directly by the 'genetic vehicle'—but, the individual is likely not free of the idea of 'bodies', much less the string of implants that seems to keep the considerations of *Alpha-Spirits* fixed to the planet Earth *once* they arrive here. And our journey on the "Backtrack" is not limited only to this planet, this galaxy, or even this version of a Universe. As such, the part of the *Pathway* treated with "Alpha-Defragmentation" is like lifting the lid on the ultimate vault; and there really is no way to cease moving forward when you're this far up the *Ladder*. By this point of realization on the "Wizard Grades" we *know* better; and how could we... why would we ever choose to go back to when we didn't *know*?

You need not fear that we are moving upward on the *Pathway* blindly. We are *backtracking* along the same routes that have brought us here. This is all familiar ground—*even* if we have wanted to forget it so much that we *have*. Because we most certainly *have* that power. But we also have the power to reclaim what we have forgotten along the way; that *Spiritual Awareness* that we have left behind on the *Backtrack,* or have a sense of "*loss*" over, as we descended to fix our **attention** on Human point-of-views. We have the ability to evolve *back* toward our natural state—returning to the Source, as it is said—and still retain the *knowingness* of the experience we have realized along the way. We can retain this *knowingness* without having to carry the heavy mementos of energetic **turbulence** as constant reminders and diversions of our *Awareness*. We can certainly realize our true *Self-hood—* our true *god-hood*—once again.

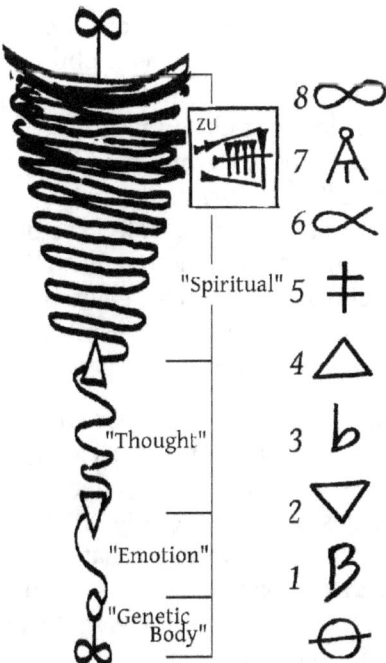

.: LECTURE TWO :.
THE QUEST FOR THE BACKTRACK
17, MARCH 2023

Before getting deep into the Systemological technicalities of the *Backtrack*, I want to take a moment to review a bit of the history behind endeavors to uncover the truth about *"past-lives."* It is not necessary to know all of the vast background to effectively apply our systematic philosophy to *Backtrack* explorations; but obviously there *was* a world out there before Systemology and we are not the first *Seekers* of this knowledge to come along. Nor do we operate in a vacuum or develop material exclusively from some ivory tower out-of-touch with what is happening elsewhere. But we are both wide-viewing *and* systematic in our approach to what is actually implemented within our Systemology.

At Grade-V, it's not particularly beneficial to scrutinize all the various differences between philosophies of metempsychosis and transmigration that have passed down the line. Each cultural tradition has relayed a communication reflecting its own flavors, its own levels of understanding, portraits of spirituality painted with various contexts of divinity—whether sole creators or administrative pantheons of **intermediaries**. The evolution of fragmented details of distorted beliefs is not as significant for our purposes as tracing down the original truths that may have inspired these concepts—if any.

We also, at each turn, must consider the audience that a communication is intended for. For example, when writing for more esoteric-oriented readers, William Walker Atkinson changes his tune slightly, affirming in his discourse on *"The Arcane Teachings"* that the progress of an upward 'Spiritual Evolution' is not evenly distributed among all persons; that the universality of an elevated state of consciousness in which to reside more permanently is not imminently guaranteed just because a person has *dropped* their body with its death. One will note that the subject of "death" comes up quite frequently when concerning the *Backtrack*. A *Seeker* should be at a point, then, that their willingness to confront the subject is quite high. Atkinson goes on to say:

> "Not all reach [Spiritual Evolution]—many fall by the wayside, or sink into the mire. The Arcane Teachings do not hold that rebirth is imposed arbitrarily, or by **reason** of punishment and rewards for deeds of the physical life; but, on the contrary, that it proceeds [systematically] following the general *Path*, the desire [goals] and character, of the Individual. The 'character' of the Individual is composed of the sum of their experience and desires [goals], and follows the line of general expression in deciding future embodiments and life.

> "Desire [goals and purposes] is the strong motive force of Life, and its urge toward expression leads an Individual into certain **channels** of rebirth. An understanding of [desire, goals and purposes] and [**Will-Intention**] enables the Individual to regulate their character so they may practically map out future lives instead of allowing them to be determined by 'blind desire' as is the case with the majority of the Human race.

> "The Arcane Teachings do not hold that rebirth must always continue along **unconscious** lines. The 'advanced soul' reaches the plane of 'Conscious Rebirth', after a certain stage is passed—and accompanying this comes the Memory of Past Lives, so that Life becomes continuous in consciousness and memory, after a certain stage of progress is attained. The 'advancing soul' develops a clearer and clearer recollection of its past lives. The dim memories, and flashes of past remembrance, which

many of us now have, will be succeeded eventually by a full remembrance of the details.

"Re-embodiment on this one planet continues only so long as the Individual is attracted by *Earth* things. When it passes beyond the attractions of *Earth,* the Individual rises to meet the attraction of worlds higher in the plane, and so on. Or, likewise, the Individual may become so engrossed that it may sink to a lower level of development in worlds even beneath our own.

"Many of us now abiding on this planet, have been drawn here by reason of having *fallen* from the higher estate of higher worlds by reason of our material longings [desire, goals and purposes]. This accounts for the feeling possessed by many that they are '*far from home*', accompanied by dim flashes of remembrance of a brighter, happier and more glorious life on some higher plane in the past."

One of the reasons an emphasis on systematic processing of the *Backtrack*—or "past-lives"—was held off until the upper-level Grades is a concern for the "**invalidation**" of a *Seeker* in any way as they are still initially building up their *Actualized Awareness* with *Beta-Defragmentation.* The "data" coming off the *Backtrack* is easy to invalidate at low-levels of *Awareness.* As such, the information is not really emphasized in our earlier works or in the more visibly public presentations of "***Mardukite Zuism.***" For example, the presentation of Earth in *Beta-Existence* as a "prison planet" in *Wizard Level-0* did not prove popular with a certain minority segment of *Seekers* and readers. They were obviously not ready to *confront* that fact.

I suppose we are actually **helping** to transform Earth into a "spiritual rehabilitation center" with our Systemology. One of our initial goals put forth over a decade ago was to develop a systematic method of establishing a generation of *"metahumans"*—the *"homo novus"* that would render the existing standard-issue considerations for *"homo sapiens"* obsolete. And this is something distinguished by the *Actualized Awareness* levels of the individual—the actual *Self*—and not particularly related to the class, race and qualities of the 'genetic vehicle' that *Self* operates. We are, again, concerned primarily with 'Spiritual Evolution'. This distinction between *Beingness* of an *Alpha-Spirit* versus a '*genetic-vehicle*' is quite **prevalent** in our Systemology since its inception. It is even more critical when we systematically distinguish a *Backtrack* for the *Alpha-Spirit* that is wholly separate from the "**genetic memory**" of a material body that has obviously followed a course of its own evolution, on its own *track*.

This distinction is not arbitrary. It is one more semantic aspect of our Systemology that is uniquely distinct from the level of understanding held by many other spiritual traditions and metaphysical philosophies. Such individuals that have difficulty realizing this distinction with clarity are still very much *over*-**identified** with material bodies. You will find this even among many in the 'New Age' movement. They say, "well, my 'DNA-test' says I'm originally from Romania, therefore..." Uh, what? My car was made in Mexico; my friend's, in Japan. What does that matter to us as drivers? Even so, the odds of an *Alpha-Spirit* sticking with one ancestral generational line of a specific **organic** body is incredibly remote. As Atkinson continues to suggest in his discourse:

> "Each Individual has been embodied in numerous personalities during its Spiritual Evolution. Old Atlantis; Chaldea; Egypt; Greece; and other ancient lands have known us. Rome; Tyre; Carthage; **Babylon**; Troy; and other cities of the past have been ours. We have worshiped Jove; Isis; Thor; Wodin; Marduk; Baal; Pan; and many other strange

gods. We have learned many lessons—we have had many defeats and many victories. And we are now emerging into a conscious realization of what it all means..."

More evidence for "organic glorification" is also rampant among metaphysical circles that speak heavily of "RH-negative" blood-types, and other genetic qualifications that only seem to serve 'elitist' purposes. But we are still talking about 'vehicles' and not any qualities concerning the actual 'driver'. Okay, so maybe they're sporting a classy *Porsche* around for a lifetime instead of a *Pinto.* But, you know, an inexperienced young driver behind the wheel of a top-of-the-line muscle car isn't exactly going to be demonstrating any great lofty and enlightened *joie de vivre.* And how enlightened is it to believe an individual cannot reach the destination of *Ascension* just because they're not driving the right car? Perhaps it's possible that some *are* better *equipped* in this lifetime to accelerate towards that goal—*but will they?*

We have quite enough to deal with regarding 'spiritual contamination' or 'fragmentation' inherent in the artificial personalities and roles taken on in various lifetimes to concern ourselves very much with the evolutionary line of a *genetic vehicle* that we, at best, make a temporary use of. And need I remind you that those of us here now in Grade-V are making temporary use of such a *vehicle* to communicate and experience game-play at the level or plane of existence we are seeking to ascend from. So, let us be sure that our priorities—our significances and importances—are in line. Let us be certain that we carry no *'hidden standards'* into our endeavor of reclaiming the *Backtrack.*

Based on the common beliefs and behaviors of the masses, it would seem like the idea of *'Spiritual Evolution'* or a continuous existence on the *Backtrack* is something incredibly new and esoteric. Most standard-issue Humans aren't living out their lives as though they have much reality on this. In spite of this—in spite of thousands of years of religious and spiritual tradition—the **apparent** reality of "past-lives" even began rearing its head in psychotherapy and parapsychology over a century ago. This idea of a continuous spiritual existence or the repeated appearances in the world using various incarnations is not born of "old wives' tales" and a few primitive practices of antiquity. It is not just a niche belief among a few **superstitious** 'New Agers'.

Even throughout history, though, it is found that such beliefs about the actual or spiritual *Self* moving on after a particular physical lifetime are more natural, innate and prevalent than its opposite. When we even consider all of the subjective accounts from those that have *almost* "died"—or experienced these so called "Near Death Experiences"—no matter how varied the details, they all seem to point to a certain truth: that our actual *Spiritual Awareness* as "*Self*" (in its basic state) is very much **exterior** to this Physical Universe and any of its considerations for *Beta-Existence*. But, of course, operating in life with this certainty does not come easily to all folks.

We seem intuitive about the subject sometimes; but often it is hidden or covered up in jest or small sentiment. The recognition of familiarity when we meet and communicate with someone. Just making contact seems to inspire in us some sense of "well, maybe we knew each other in another life." What is it that we are recognizing on a higher level of realization? Because certainly it is not the newly incarnated physical shell that we see before us at *this* level of material contact and communication. Or, consider those romantic couples that believe themselves some type or another of "Twin Flame" that will go on to remain together "in the next life." Of course, we all have our own course to travel; but is all of this simply wishful thinking or is there something valid underlying it?

Then we have that concept that some refer to as the "Old Soul"—which Atkinson refers to, probably more accurately, as an "Advanced Soul"—which pops up here and there. This generally is used to refer to someone that is more observably 'awakened' or carrying increased 'Actualized Awareness'; because **chronologically**, everyone has been around for quite a while. At our best estimate, an Alpha-Spirit has been experiencing various existences in various universes for four-quadrillion years, relatively speaking. If we were to take the estimated age of this version of Beta-Existence or Physical Universe at fifteen-billion years as just one example, that would leave a Being enough time to experience the entire **extant** life of not only this Universe, but over a quarter-of-a-million Universes just like it. Of course, we would not expect the "lifespan" of each Universe to be equal—or our participation or attendance equal in each. But, this is simply to illustrate the mathematical magnitude of what we are really talking about in our metaspirituality.

Given the last 6,000 years of Human history, it is interesting to see that the "you only live once" mantra, and other religious dogma about permanent etheric destinations in the afterlife, occur relatively recently. Enforced spiritual doctrine on "Heaven and Hell" seemed to increase proportional to the amount of **control** and wealth sought by the Catholic Church—and, of course, it propagated this doctrine to the other protestant denominations that split away from it. But, curiously, we do not see this same dogmatic emphasis present in the original teachings of Jesus Christ. In fact, records show that a few hundred years after his death, many references to "reincarnation" were removed from the texts that we would later come to know as the "Holy Bible." But, obviously, the spiritual minds of his time must have been aware that the phenomenon exists. One of the first things they ask him is "if he is Elijah"—they factually inquire if he is a reincarnated prophet returned!

You would think with all the talk of *eternal spirits*, that folks would have a better reality on the matter. Critics, or else those ignorant, of the reality of the *Backtrack*, often argue that a belief in multiple lives causes an individual to be less *ethical* in their dealing. They think it implies a belief that nothing matters because you can just come back and do it all over again, or something. This is a bit ironic, because I have found that those with a greater reality on it actually exhibit *more* **ethics** in their handling of life. We don't really even have to bring any technicalities of "*karma*" in on this. It's not difficult to realize that if we do return here on Earth: the world we are living in today, the **manifestation** of our thoughts and actions today—this is what we are going to be facing tomorrow. Each of us, even on a material level, based on what is happening "*in here*," is participating in the creation of what is perceived as the reality "*out there*" all the way along the *track*.

Λ Δ Δ Δ Δ Δ Δ

Systemology is not the first applied philosophy to discover therapeutic value in what the professionals refer to as "past-life regression." Many spiritual ministers, psychoanalysts, New Thought practitioners and mystics have all encountered some kind of reality on the subject. The general **consensus** has been that if it yields effective results —if a *Seeker* were to get better—then they should run with it. Even the psychology papers affirm that regardless of what the beliefs or actuality of the "spiritual" situation may be, if an individual is improved by handling "past-life" memory, then it is at least as applicable or clinically effective as what we systematically apply as "imaginative" or "creative ability" processing.

A *Seeker* that has worked thoroughly through the *Beta-Defragmentation* regimen of earlier Grades—as outlined in "*Systemology-180*"—may discover a few shortcomings in their progress in certain areas. And this is not an over-sight or a deficiency on the techniques or the training for those levels of work. Remember: the right tool for the right job. So, with "Route-4"—the *Backtrack*—we are resolving more of the turbulent energy that is still wrapped up with a *Seeker*, aspects of life that still hold a tremendous **charge** that didn't seem to get resolved in the standard techniques.

One of the reasons certain aspects do not resolve in standard *Beta-Defragmentation* is the original focus we had on "staying within the boundaries of *this* lifetime." Rather than bring additional training and information into play concerning the *Backtrack*, we decided to system-atically apply "**imagination**" and "creativeness" pro-cessing in *Wizard Level-0* as an alternative. *Seekers* were still running into the *Backtrack* because much of the im-agery imagined, and not *recalled* from *this* life, restimu-lated scenes and **imprinting** incurred on the *Backtrack*.

Quite frankly, in spite of the numerous experiences, *im-printing incidents* and **emotional encoding** encountered during a *Seeker's* present lifetime, most of it pales consid-erably compared with what it is being *added on to* from the *Backtrack*. This phenomenon can get in the way of reaching a point of stable *Beta-Defragmentation*—because fragmentation that occurs in this life is being compoun-ded with the fragmentation that already exists on the line. And there is a lot that we have picked up on our long journey to this point on the *track*. So to finally an-swer the burning question for *Pilots*: yes, the energetic **turbulence** that does not seem to discharge when focus-ing on this lifetime, or using "imagination" techniques, very likely stems from earlier on the *Backtrack*.

Most of the time, the course that a person is on in this lifetime, the roles and goals they pursue, is the result of "past-life" and "between-life" *implanted* goals. There are many large cycles that play out on the *Backtrack*: where an individual is at first playing at one game and then they are playing against it; or they are at first assuming one type of role, and then deciding that another type would be preferred, will suddenly switch courses on the matter. And this runs for many, many lifetimes and displays various patterns that can even allow us to predict behaviors and synchronize processing emphasis based on where a *Seeker* is at within those cycles. All of this is, for us, treated quite systematically for Grade-V—just as one should expect from Systemology.

There are many appearances of "past-life regression" techniques in contemporary 'New Age' literature. Many of them involve "between" states, such as *trance* or *dream-work.* I've mentioned the "Near Death Experience" example previously, but there are also other points when an individual is consciously "detached" from exclusively considering from the **POV** of a body; particularly in extreme cases. One doesn't have to necessarily stop breathing; there are other states such as extreme *fever* or some form of sensory deprivation (or desensitization) that have sparked momentary glimpses of the "*Other.*" Many have attempted to employ *meditation* to achieve similar states and spiritual insights. So, we are not unleashing a revolutionary new subject with the *Backtrack,* but we are taking a more systematic approach to the work than what most other spiritual traditions and mystical practices have done.

My own 'New Age' introduction to the subject involved practical exercises using a pendulum, maps and various lists. There is something to that technique, but the same principles could be applied with a *GSR-Meter* and get faster, more concise, results. So, that has been my own preferred method—and that is presented in Grade-V as "*Route-4G.*" Of course, the most commonly cited method in the 'New Age' and fields of "creative psychology" regard use of *hypnosis* in their therapy. If a *Seeker* is properly "in session" providing "presence"—has contacted objects in the environment, is able to process basic recall and so forth—then there is certainly no need to employ *hypnosis* for systematic processing.

There is a lot of material out there to satisfy intellectual curiosity. Most of what you will find are simply narratives of some person's account about this or that. Anything like that really didn't serve of much value when developing the Systemology of the *Backtrack*. However, some of the various 'New Age' manuals and psychological papers can provide some useful basic details to a *Pilot*, such as the advice given by Florence McClain in her book on "*Past Life Regression*" from the 1980's, where she says:

> "While conducting a regression, accept whatever answers are given to your questions. Do not question or argue with the answers. This is not part of your function. Also, be careful that you do not ask leading questions, even if you have impressions of what the person regressing is seeing or experiencing. If the person is not getting clear impressions about his or her surroundings, for instance, and you are, do not ask, 'Are you in a house?'—instead, maybe ask, 'Are you inside some structure or outdoors? Are you in the country, a village, small town or large city?' Give them the choice and their minds will focus on the right answer. Keep the person observing and conversing..."

Δ Δ Δ Δ Δ Δ

"Route-4" *Backtrack* work and other forms of *recall* in systematic processing are not really regression sessions in the traditional clinical sense—but they do contact some of the same aspects of life concerning memory and energetic turbulence. Another difference between our Systemology and these other traditional approaches is the manner in which the data is processed systematically in order to improve the *Seeker*. There is a considerable difference between the type of exploratory processing one might do for research and the type of defragmentation processing that is issued as a gradient toward *Ascension*. For example, at the Systemology Society, our research methods differ from the actual results that are provided in the Grades and published for the purposes of increasing an individual's *Actualized Awareness*.

The type of work found elsewhere reflects the type of exercises and techniques explored at *Wizard Level-0* and below. For example, the *regression meditation* suggested by McClain, which is quite similar to the techniques used by *Freud* and *Carl Jung*, begins with an extensive relaxation and breathing technique before employing "imagination" and "visualization" to access **circuits** in the mind. We have made use of such techniques formerly at other gradients. Many of them involving the use of iconic imagery—doorways, gates, **thresholds** of some kind—to access some type of mental experience. For those who *are* interested in experimenting with this approach, McClain's suggested script is easily able to be directed by any Class-3D *Pilot*, if so desired. It reads:

> "Imagine that you are standing in front of the door to your home. Imagine that you are opening the door. Imagine that the door opens into a long tunnel and that you can see a light at the end of the tunnel. I am going to count from *twenty* to *one*. With each descending number imagine that you are moving down the tunnel toward the light and moving back through time to a lifetime you lived previous to this one. At the count on *one* you will step from the tunnel into the light, into a lifetime which you lived previous to this one."

And then there is the descending countdown, slowly, repeating some of the former affirmations with the count to reinforce the instructions. Then:

> "*One.* You are now in a lifetime you lived previous
> to this one. Mentally look out through your eyes
> and listen through your ears. Mentally look down
> at your feet. What are you wearing on your feet?"

Of course, the *Pilot* or a person running the regression
would want to pause briefly to wait for responses for
each of the questions; engaging in greater two-way communication wherever appropriate.

> "What are you wearing on your body. About what
> age are you? Are you male or female? What is your
> name, the first name which comes to mind? Men-
> tally look through our eyes and listen through your
> ears. Where are you? Describe your surroundings.
> What part of the world are you in? Do you know
> what year or time period it is?"

Then, she asks about family and relatives to orient the
person into the life—the type of questions a *Pilot* might
issue for a preliminary interview before working with a
new *Seeker.* An individual in regression can also quickly
Back-Scan a sample day in that life.

> "How do you spend your time? [Now,] move for-
> ward in time to a point where you are approxim-
> ately *five* years older, about the age of [such and
> such]. It will only take a moment. You will feel
> time passing around you like currents of air or
> pages flipping off a calendar. Tell me as soon as
> you are there. Mentally look out through your eyes
> and listen through your ears..."

And she lists a whole series of sample questions. Most of
the scripts for regression techniques that we analyzed at
the Systemology Society ran along similar lines. So, my
intention for giving you this is really to demonstrate
what is out there; what other people have been doing.

Other than Grade-V instruction and the information pulled directly from the *Backtrack,* this is the type of material that a *Seeker* or *Pilot* is likely to find if they decide to go out and explore this subject more elsewhere. There isn't a lot else out there except an endless string of "case studies" and regression narratives.

While I may not have covered every historical detail here in this short review of the background, I believe we have adequately introduced the subject of "past-lives" enough to get this Spring 2023 lecture series *on track*—no pun intended.

.: LECTURE THREE :.
SYSTEMOLOGY-180 & THE BACKTRACK
18, MARCH 2023

Previous Systemology work **differentiated** between the organic-body system we refer to as the '*genetic-vehicle*' and the Spiritual Awareness Unit that is actually *you*, which we call the *Alpha-Spirit*. Even when I wrote "*Systemology: The Original Thesis*" back in 2010, I had a sense for what Systemology would specifically have to entail—I just didn't know how far we would actually have to run with it.

Many seekers have already run into the *Backtrack* during *Beta-Defragmentation*, which is one of many reasons why I compiled the "*Systemology-180*" volume for Grade-V. It actually consists of all the practical or technical data from Grade-III and Grade-IV, but it is actually quite relevant for upper-level work. We started talking about "*Sys-180*" a couple of years ago; but of course, Grade-IV had to be completed to my satisfaction before we could compile a manual and officially announce a total *Beta-Defragmentation* regimen and move on to other areas for the Wizard Grades. Basic foundations of this upper-level work are still just as critical, and even directly applicable to the *Backtrack*, so long as we aren't restricting our focus to *this* lifetime.

This *life*, and this version of *Beta-Existence*, is but a '**microcosm**' of the same games and tendencies that take place at higher levels of reality earlier on the *Backtrack*—and which ultimately brought us to the considerations and postulates of the here and now. Therefore, most of the basic Systemology research work concerning the *Backtrack* actually took place synchronously with the earlier Grades, but remained intentionally separate. Even in the original "*Reality Engineering*" workshops for Systemology in 2013, I was referring to the "Mind-of-Body" as distinct from, and lower in order to, the "Mind-of-Spirit"—but this was before I had more thoroughly worked out the "**Standard Model**" we use today.

In Systemology, we treat the physical body or *genetic-vehicle* as a distinct entity—a living organism—that is independent of the *Alpha-Spirit*. The *genetic-vehicle* has its own cellular or genetic memory that is wholly separate from our own, but it obviously plays a part or has an effect on the body—and therefore, our experiences with using a body. Just as the *Alpha-Spirit* has a recorded memory of its own *Backtrack,* so too does the *genetic-vehicle*, though it is much cruder and carried much closer to the organism —right in its very cells of life. And again, this is not so different from the automation involved in an *Alpha-Spirit* being imprinted with impressions that dictate reasoning to support survival. Thus, again, a closer, or wider-angle, view on what we have already learned in former Grades can reveal a lot of what we should expect concerning systems, **phases** and cycles for the *Backtrack.*

In Grade-III, we introduce the Standard Model, which includes an understanding of two distinct points on the ZU-line: the "***Reactive Control Center***" or **RCC** at "2.0"; and the "***Master Control Center***" or **MCC** at "4.0"—and these would be, respectively, what I considered the "Mind-of-Body" and the "Mind-of-Spirit" over a decade ago. The RCC is that which the '*genetic-vehicle*' is carrying, and the memory it stores concerning physical survival of its organic body. The MCC is the networked circuitry that the *Alpha-Spirit* is toting along from one incarnation to the next—and in between material lifetimes. Both are systematic constructs compulsively created and duplicated through time; neither *is* the actual *Self;* combined they are the intermediary relay station for experiencing energetic communications (and commands) between the *Alpha-Spirit* and the *genetic-vehicle.*

The *genetic-vehicle* possesses systematic **faculties** that keep it alive in the absence of an *Alpha-Spirit*. If it did not —if it was not able to maintain a basic level of survival independent of an *Alpha-Spirit*—it would not remain living during periods experienced as "**biological-unconsciousness**." During such periods, the *Awareness* of the *Alpha-Spirit* is ejected to a point-of-view *exterior* to the *genetic-vehicle*; and it is such that prompts a greater certainty on the independence and longevity of the *Spirit*. During periods of biological unconsciousness, the *genetic-vehicle* is still very much alive and making a sensory record of its **perceptions**.

Understand that in our view—in Systemology—the evolution of the *Alpha-Spirit* is not confused with the evolution of organic life on Earth or in this Universe. Both are continually evolving, in the strictest sense of the word, but on completely separate *tracks*. This is where the **dichotomy** of science and religion is settled as a non-problem. Where the two cross, you have a phenomenon such as the experience of an incarnation in a Human life. The basic truth has even been obscured in other forms of spirituality where they teach a message that "man is a body that *has* a soul" rather than "man *is* a soul that has a body." It seems like the understanding has been mixed up for quite a while. Which is why I've always said that our Systemology is not really presenting brand-new concepts, but a new higher-order understanding of what is right in front of us. To dissipate the confusions; and perhaps create a few new ones along the way as we tread forth in exploring the remainder of the *Pathway*; but they will be temporary, at the very least, and not the same confusions that have been fouling up the Human Condition for the past several thousand years.

The only reason that the *genetic-vehicle* is of interest to us in systematic processing at Grade-V and above is because the *imprints* stored at the level of the RCC that are *not* from *this* lifetime are very likely based on *encoding* during the evolution of the *genetic-vehicle* and not the *Alpha-Spirit*. The *Alpha-Spirit* has also experienced its own enforced *implants* and other *imprinting incidents* along its own *track*, but these are stored by the MCC, the part of the Mind-System that is actually carried by the *Alpha-Spirit* on its journey, and of which is only temporarily integrated with the *genetic-vehicle* during that period of incarnation.

For some *Seekers*—and certainly many individuals that have explored "past-lives"—the **mental imagery** of the *imprints* from either *track* are indistinguishable. But, **differentiation** is important when assigning significances. The *implants* and aspects of the MCC are much more critical to our *Ascension* work, because it is that which pertains to the actual *Self*, and thus of *real* benefit to the *Alpha-Spirit* beyond this one life here. It is important to realize that we are not processing a "body" with our systematic techniques; we are assisting an *Alpha-Spirit*, the actual individual themselves that is *using* a body. Even when we employ **"objective** exercises" that move the body, it is to systematically increase the level of skill and certainty on the individual's **control** *of* the body.

If we want to be technical about organic life, each "cell" is a living organism with its own consciousness center—a point of *Awareness*—and a point-of-view **internal** to this Physical Universe. It may even be considered that each *cell* is an *entity* unto itself and the *genetic-vehicle* is the product of cellular evolution of many living *entities* all working their parts systematically to provide for a functioning "body." These particular *entities* seem to be of a much lower-order or level of *Awareness* than the *Alpha-Spirit* that takes command of the *genetic-vehicle* as a whole.

It may even be that the Human body is composed of cellular fragments of a particular powerful being long ago on Earth that continue to propagate (and to some extent, degrade or decay) based on their own cellular programming to evolve in continuance of its own survival. This would account for some origin myths in **Mesopotamia** and elsewhere that speak of some manner of "genetic intervention" that seemed to set the Human Condition apart from all other forms of life on this planet. And this idea that Humans are *made* in "God's image"—well, seldom are they ever talking about the actual *Spirit*, so that must be some kind of reference to the *body*. Because that's the only thing being *made* down here that is to look anything like something else that might have appeared down here—and we are obviously dealing with something material and not truly spiritual or *etheric* in nature by Systemology standards. At any rate, I would have to believe all this is what is alluded to on the **cuneiform** tablets, when we read from the "*Anunnaki Bible*" that the Anunnaki Council decreed:

> "We shall prepare a purification bath. First, let one god be sacrificed and the rest cleansed by baptism. Let *Ninti* mix the clay with the sacrificed god's flesh and blood. From the flesh of the god, let a spirit remain until the End of Days. And let it be known to the living gods by the sign marked—or else he will be allowed to be forgotten, so let the spirit remain.

> "*Ninti* mixed the clay with the flesh and blood of *Awmelu*. The seed of god and man were thoroughly mixed into the clay. To the *Adamu* (which is, to say, 'Humans') they sought to bestow the face of the gods. From the flesh of the god, the spirit remained to the End of Days."

∆ ∆ ∆ ∆ ∆ ∆ ∆

Seekers began encountering the *Backtrack* with systematic processing starting from the beginning with "**Route-1**" in 2019, which we published in "*The Tablets of Destiny*" (*Liber-One*). This provided a launch point for upper-level

"*Metaspiritual*" Systemology, even while we continued to pursue the goals of the earlier Grades. But as this phenomenon continued with the release of "*Crystal Clear*" (**Liber-2B**), and the need to better handle our methodology of applying systematic processing increased, we presented more refined instructions as "Route-1 Revised" in newer copies of *Liber-One,* which began printing in late 2022 as "*The Tablets of Destiny Revelation.*" Additional behind-the-scenes work on the Wizard Grades is what primarily prompted this revision—and it is also the version provided in our new "*Systemology-180*" volume for Grade-V.

"*Systemology-180*" is of particular interest to *Seekers* that have already collected earlier experimental releases of our material, but still want to benefit from the revised instruction we are now able to offer—now that we have had several more years of critical development on the subject. "*Systemology-180*" is also a critical point for Grade-V, where we are *looking back* and reviewing the stable data and effective techniques that have delivered us to this point. We are also reexamining the material from Grade-III and Grade-IV with a new perspective—and obviously that includes taking the *Backtrack* into account.

One of the greatest concerns with releasing a title like "*Systemology-180*" is that it inspires attempts at "*Flying Solo*"—what we used to call "Self-Processing"—without adequate *Pilot* training. This is a greater concern primarily with those that discover it as, for example, their first book on Systemology. And perhaps one of the risks there, is the danger of invalidation. An individual picks it up, has no background in the theory of its development or use, and decides it's no good; tells his friends and family it's no good. I mean—you give some construction plans for an "atomic super-collider" to a two-year old and they're not going to know what to do with them either. It would be of no relative or comprehended value to them;

but it can mean something and be of actual use to someone else.

In view of the fact that most of those *Seekers* exploring Systemology apart from the Mardukite Academy do so by themselves or with a few close ones, but primarily seem to be *"Flying Solo"* on their exercises, it seems appropriate to provide some *Pilot* training with that in mind. It's actually been a couple of years since I directly addressed the subject of "Self-Processing" in the lectures* of 2019. Afterward, we were focusing on *cooperative* use of systemological techniques for the Academy. In spite of that, over the years, many solitary *Seekers* have still yielded positive gains and stable results using the material.

Pilot training is critical for solitary *Seekers* because it allows them to avoid some of the more common pitfalls of applying so-called "Self-Help" techniques. Grade-IV details concerning a *"professional piloting session"*—such as in **SOP-2C**—may be employed to provide structure for someone working alone. Very often the type of solitary processing that is not yielding results is often operated without applying proper *"presence"* to the session, or working on the wrong gradient, or incomplete cycles of work, or simply in the wrong direction on the wrong **terminals.** We sought to avoid this when developing the **"Creative Ability Training"** regimen for Wizard Level-0, which proved quite effective for solitary *Seekers,* but that material also presented and emphasized a different style of technique than other Routes.

Systematic Processing is not directed toward the body, or even directly to the Mind-System—it is a communication with the individual—the *Self* or *Alpha-Spirit*—who in turn is commanding the Mind-System and operations of a body. This is just as true when an individual is *"Flying Solo."* As such, the **"processing command lines"**—or

---

* Serving as the basis for *"Crystal Clear"* (*Liber-2B*).

PCLs—seldom need to be spoken verbally or out loud. There has been some misconceptions about being able to run PCLs silently; and if a *Seeker* is working alone, they most definitely should. A *Seeker* should also only be focused on one "command line" at a time. If using written materials, then a sheet of paper can be used to cover other lines on the page. Another option that we use quite often for training and other exercises is to write out each PCL intended for use on their own index card.

Δ Δ Δ Δ Δ Δ

Although the techniques and exercises of *Beta-Defragmentation* seemed to mostly pertain to the more 'physical' and 'mental' systems of the Human Condition, our approach in Grade-V allows us to focus our attention more directly on the '*Spiritual Timeline*' that extends back behind us nearly infinitely. We are still dealing with a "Mind" construct, because apparently that plays a hand in our maintaining this *track* sequentially behind us with such rigidity.

An experienced *Seeker* is also aware that when we are '**processing-out**' the turbulent energy stores that are fixed to some **channel** or *circuit*, we are not actually "erasing" the *Knowingness* or literal "memory" of an incident, event or *mental image*; we are reducing, releasing and eliminating the accumulated *charge* that forms an energetic "*mass*" or solid blockage on what should otherwise be a free-**flowing** current. This is why, when a thick "field" of solidity or wave-ridges surround a particular channel of thought, the increased resistance is actually detectible in subtle changes in the electrical field that surrounds the body, which the *Alpha-Spirit* **projects**—and which shows up particularly well in *GSR-Metering*.

But in regards to Grade-V *Piloting* and the *Backtrack*, we are operating on the premise that the actual *Self* or *Alpha*

Spirit goes on in its spiritual existence beyond this life-time. Thus, we can **logically** affirm that the *Spirit* has also experienced previous incarnations of *Beingness* before this present "lifetime"—and as such, there must obviously be something that blocks the fluid recall of it, once fixing our attention of *Beingness* to the standard-issue Human Condition. This blockage causes many individuals to invalidate the existence of "past-lives"—even among many religions that seem to simultaneously profess that the *Spirit* is *eternal.*

The *Pathway to Ascension* as presented in Systemology is also based on a premise that we are "reclaiming" something which has been lost—or forgotten—to us; and not that we are taking on some newly acquired realizations or spiritual abilities for the first time. The *ascent* that we are retracing is consequential to the fact that we have *descended.* Whatever "god-like" state we maintained at our Source, we have certainly strayed far and distant from it to find ourselves in such a trapped condition. Our spiritual journey certainly did not begin *down here*—and certainly not with *this* lifetime.

My goal in presenting the "*Backtrack*" lectures is not to convince anyone of anything or about the reality of *past-lives.* A *Seeker* that has progressed to Grade-V and *Wizard Level-1* doesn't usually require convincing on the subject. The matter presents itself at a time when a *Seeker* is actually ready and willing to confront it—or at least some part of it, since we are handling the *Backtrack* on a gradient scale, just as we did the preliminary regimen of *Beta-Defragmentation.* Because these "blockages" were obviously accumulated systematically over the course of the *track.* The nature of "fragmentation" concerns aspects that have been *added* to ones sense of a 'Spiritual Timeline'—or even the Mind-System—rather than as a result of some innate deficiency or lack.

Our perception of the "Divine" within Systemology is

rooted in the original *Arcane Tablets* describing an "Infinity of Nothingness"—but a Nothing with the infinite **potential** for creation; and hence each *Alpha-Spirit* is a fragment of this at its truest and most basic state. This **Alpha**-state for *Self* would be a "static" point as a unit of pure *'Spiritual Awareness'*—defined as "**ZU**" in the very first written language at the start of this cycle of recorded history or version of civilization on Earth. And certainly there have been other versions of civilization that have come and gone from the planet; our acute knowledge of them, archaeologically speaking, being restricted to the extent that their communications survive. And our own written history for this cycle is only 6,000 years old at best, leaving much room for traditional scientific speculation on the remainder.

As a colleague so concisely pointed out to me years ago: the nature of our descent as beings of infinite potential would consist of postulated *denials* of the same; that the blockages would be considerations against our true nature. These would include the decisions that result from excessive or compulsive *withdrawal*—because a being of infinite potential would thereafter have to make decisions not to create; not to communicate; not to perceive or experience; and by perfect reflection with the type of behavior mirrored in the Human Condition, the decision to *not-know*. And based on that very true nature we possess, anything that is created for the *reality* of our personal universe must in some way be agreed to—and then is compulsively created by us in perpetuity.

This whole concept is actually the main subject of Michael Crichton's book and film titled "*Sphere.*" In this piece, a group of isolated Humans are suddenly the effect of their own spontaneously manifested **thought-forms**. They have the power awakened in them to essentially have things "be" or "not be" at will; but of course that "will" is surprisingly fragmented by their inability to manage emotions and "**unconscious**" thought. Their only solution to not destroying each other is to *use* the "power" to *forget* they have the *ability* altogether. And we discovered in *Wizard Level-1* that an individual's inability to manage emotion and reactive thought—to handle **responsibility** for their creations—progressively across the *Backtrack,* has actually led to the apparent diminished *'Spiritual Ability'* maintained among the standard-issue Human Condition today. Luckily, we can still *retrace* our steps—and reclaim it.

Seekers, particularly those operating solitary, run the same risk as *magicians* and *mystics* that allow their attentions to remain on an incomplete process. This is probably one of the more important aspects of *Pilot* training: to recognize or gauge the effects from running a process. Since running things too long is a bit more difficult for a solo-*Pilot* to correct, and getting hung-up on any one thing is generally more frustrating when alone than skipping it for one cycle and coming back to it, our advice for "Self-Processing" has always been to move through it at a comfortable pace and cycle back over it again later.

While what I've said is still true of the Wizard Grades and the *Backtrack,* at these upper-levels, it is more critical that a *Seeker* not "pass by" or "bypass" any turbulent *charge* once it is found. It is difficult to describe what is "happening" with a *Seeker* during processing. It is probably better equated to a *feeling.* By Grade-V, a *Seeker* has experienced what it's like to be *really flying* on a process that is yielding positive results. So, if something really starts happening with a process, the only course of action is to complete it. Once a *Seeker* has accumulated too many "half-run" exercises, progress on the *Pathway* slows down or stops altogether. And if one's personal defragmentation is not handled progressively, for example, using the Grades and Routes provided, then the more advanced work becomes more difficult to run, takes too long, or the *Seeker* doesn't have enough understanding of the technique to make it effective. In the end, if something *is* "bypassed," then the only course of action is to go back and finish what you started before moving on to something else. It really isn't *more* complicated then *that.*

Systematic processing *defragments* by peeling back layers of *imprints* and *programming.* Even within a single processing technique, results occur as seeming incremental layers. For example, when running through an incident, more information and detail seems to become apparent—and we are in a position to notice things that we might have missed; or it triggers an earlier incident on a "chain" of similar incidents that have been all compounded together. The total realization of a process is not likely to be reached with a single run of a "command line"—and so this is what we mean about leaving things unfinished. Until the point of completion—so long as something is "happening" or new answers are being originated—you keep running it.

Our Systemology is an *applied philosophy*—and that means "doing" things. The days of the old stuffy long-bearded elitist philosophers sitting around a table drunkenly debating have been played out. There is a certain *sense* involved with systematic processing that is really only earned through experience; through the actual *application* of the philosophy. And we only expect an individual to do this to the extent that they can reach from the gradient they are reaching from. There is a certain point in working with all this material regularly when things just seem to sort of "click"—and suddenly there is a greater sense of what is to be accomplished and how to handle it. And this, of course, comes from practice.

Completion of a process should provide some sense of relief, if emotional turbulence has been discharged or some other realization has been reached. Depending on the duration of the session leading to this point, it is often better to end that particular session and take a break before continuing on to a new process. And by process we mean an actual process along the Routes. At first, learning the earlier techniques to get into contact with the environment, or provide "presence" to a session, will seem like entire processes in themselves and may initially take the equivalency of an entire session to actually have a reality on. Later on down the line with practice, these techniques take less session time and allow a *Seeker* to provide more attention—or *Actualized Awareness*—to the running of some other process.

The same "objective"-style techniques and positive "recall" used to orient a *Seeker* in a session are the same "emergency" applications a *Seeker* can apply by themselves if the turbulence encountered is suddenly too great or there is an incredible feeling of overwhelm. This is a greater risk when processing is handled by an inexperienced *Pilot* or a *Seeker* that is *Flying-Solo*; but in actuality, it can happen anytime you are 'stirring' things up in the Mind—and what's most important is that it's handled. In this case, a *Seeker's Self-directed Attention*. When working alone, it's also okay to end off to let things cool down for a while before revisiting whatever stirred up turbulence.

Good and thorough systemological training can also assist in developing skills of being able to *spot* what may have gone wrong in processing and correct it. One of the more common issues is attempting to apply "presence" to a certain process when attention is actually elsewhere, meaning a *Seeker* is distracted. This can even occur when aspects of the *genetic-vehicle* are affecting concentration, such as physical discomfort, lethargy, hunger or thirst. Things like that. Obviously, systematic processing along the Routes produces the most progress when a *Seeker* is feeling their best, with *Awareness* at least at analytical levels, and a positive interest in their own "*path.*" When a

Seeker isn't feeling *100%*, it's better to focus on techniques that will improve this in *present-time* rather than straining to reach higher vistas.

Sometimes a *Seeker* is able to provide enough *presence* to get a session started, but then for whatever reason they get distracted or interrupted before completing a process. In this case, you'll want to retrace your steps over the last several exercises that were used and finish off any incompleteness. It is also important to actually understand the Route training associated with a technique, as well as any words used in the "command line" for a process. Misunderstood words and instructions will certainly hold up progress on the *Pathway*.

Another concern that I've already mentioned briefly, which is common particularly among more inexperienced *Pilots*, is the matter of *"overrun."* This means *running* a process longer than what is necessary to yield the intended results. For example, a *Seeker* has already achieved the positive **end-point** for that cycle of work, but they keep grinding away at it anyways; and the more positive mood or state that was attained starts to diminish. The practical remedy for this is to stop running it, *spot* the point that the process was completed and you were feeling better about it and return attention and *Awareness* to *that* point. You see, if you're using our *Tech* and get into trouble, you can use it to get out of it, too. If you start mixing in a lot of other practices and concepts, it becomes more challenging to work out what part of our work a *Seeker* found difficulties with.

One of the issues that I'm running into more and more with the public release of this Systemology work at higher gradients, is that readers have access to materials before they are really ready to confront them. But I am still keeping these communication lines open for the developmental grades. The general consensus is that once we pierce the upper-most goals of, for example, Grade-VII, we probably will only release the material directly to individuals personally, by mail or such. I would expect that the public presentation of Systemology materials as mass-distributed books will end off with Grade-VI. And even that is pushing things because some have expressed concern about even presenting Grade-VI publicly. But this is not something that we have to immediately concern ourselves with here at Grade-V.

Hopefully some of the advice I've provided here can be used to some benefit by you in considering the systematic processing of *fragmentation* on any level—*alpha* or *beta*. These tips and tidbits are really meant to increase the effectiveness you are experiencing with the work. It's not intended to be a whole thing about "rules" and such; but rather to make sure a *Seeker* or *Pilot* is well versed and practiced in the fundamentals—because it is these basic aspects that tend to get missed; and then an individual is expecting some "magic words" of a "command line" to remedy it—and that isn't how this works.

In Grade-V we are dealing with a "spiritual **imperative**" that pervades all work on the *Backtrack*. Up until this point, many of the techniques and teachings are beneficial to an individual, when run properly, regardless of their beliefs about existence *beyond* this lifetime. So, any *Seeker* pressing forward on the *Pathway* should at the very least have experience with applying Grade-III and Grade-IV to *this* lifetime. After experiencing those results, they should be in a better position to pursue the 'Spiritual Timeline' of their whole *track* as a spiritual being; and doing so does require having some reality on *Self* being an *Alpha-Spirit* and not a *genetic-vehicle*. With that barrier crossed, there is no reason a *Seeker* cannot benefit from further applying the *Tech* to the entire **continuum** of spiritual experience—and that is what we are doing now.

.: LECTURE FOUR :.
FIRST STEPS ON THE BACKTRACK
("ROUTE-4A" & "ROUTE-3Θ")
18, MARCH 2023

Interestingly, although we transitioned to Grade-V progressively up from Grade-IV, our first steps on the *Backtrack* share greater similarity to how we went into Grade-III and the treatment of the present incarnation. By this, I mean that the first techniques I'm providing here are a development that came out of "Route-2." Of course, I like to start these Grades off with some kind of lecture series that presents and introduces the Grade and what led up to that current **tier**. This usually results in a basic textbook that is later supplemented with a more practical "workbook"-style guide toward progressing at *that* same tier.

When Systemology was brought up from the underground with Grade-III in 2019, the heart of the lecture material is what you find reworked as *"Tablets of Destiny (Revelation)" (Liber-One)*, and then supplemented thereafter with a collection of exercises and training presented as *"Crystal Clear" (Liber-2B)*. Of course, with Grade-IV, we had the first Professional Piloting Course in 2020 as the basis of the *"Metahuman Destinations"* volumes, which we then brought to an apex in 2021 with the *"Imaginomicon" (Liber-3D)* workbook.

Needless to say, what is presented at this weekend conference will not be the full extent of Grade-V work. However, we have been following a tradition these past several years of developing the more user-friendly workbook supplement as a result of what we find happening with *Seekers* after initially delivering some foundation. So, this is what can be expected. Keep in mind that we are still charting this *Pathway* at the Systemology Society. Much of it seems so second-nature now, when looking back at the journey, for example, in *Systemology-180*. But understand that the way forward, for us, has been both systematic and meticulous in its real-time development. A couple years from now, at the completion, we may look back at the map we have charted—and all these books and stuff—and say, *"yeah, but of course."* But those of us *now* that have been *in it*—forging ahead, blazing a trail—it has certainly been some very intensive, but very rewarding, research and development work to get this far, and to get here with any stable *certainty*.

The first Route-4 exercises I want to share with you are effective "first steps" on the *Backtrack,* so long as a *Seeker* has an understanding and experience with "*Analytical Recall*" in Route-2. Now, *this isn't* "analytical recall" or we would just tack it on to Route-2. But the operation of it as a "systematic process" is very similar to what you find in "*Crystal Clear*" for Grade-III—because, at the end of the day, we *are* dealing with *recall,* which is the act of remembrance. Naturally, we want *Seekers* to improve their certainty on recall with *this* life, that is obviously more accessible, before presenting the *Backtrack*.

Unlike the more "objective" techniques that handle *presence* in a present-time environment, ultimately the *Backtrack* requires "subjectively" confronting the past. Again, a *Seeker* has earned some practice in increasing willingness and skill in this area in previous Grades. We've also learned a thing or two about how to handle **traumatic** *incident reduction* from earlier work as well. And in this case, as in Route-2 and such, the best way of starting out is not to immediately jump into the heaviest incidents and risk restimulating all that circuitry, including aspects that may be above a *Seeker's* present level of *Actualized Awareness.* Eventually, the heavy turbulence and build up of energetic masses or *implants* and such do need to be handled for *Alpha-Defragmentation,* but it is certainly not the first steps.

One trick to this is starting out with what is considered positive or pleasant in one's past. While *fragmentation* is often tied to energetic turbulence and other **entangle-ment**—which is worked out and essentially *reduced* or *discharged* when handled with appropriately targeted attention in systematic processing—those aspects of our life that are truly pleasant will never diminish in their ability to provide a sense of "strength" when encountering the unpleasant. Sure, they can be masked and shrouded in a way that we can momentarily forget, but they never cease to be there for us. At any time that running an *imprinting* or *implanting* incident becomes overwhelming, a *Seeker* needs only to *spot* that positive point again. I realize this sounds like something from out of "*Peter Pan,*" but it has proved reliable—particularly as a saving grace to *Solo-Pilots* that are unable to benefit from *Co-Pilot* assistance.

Contacting positive and pleasant moments on the *track* is also helpful to increasing the willingness to actually *view* the past again. Most incidents that are unpleasant, well, a person doesn't like to *look.* And unfortunately, the way the Mind-System has been constructed, too much gets set on automatic and forgotten about. So, at first, a person is deciding that they don't want to *see* something and then by putting energy into that postulate or consideration, they get to a point where they really *don't.* For Grade-V, we have examined the basic mechanisms that are in operation in *this* lifetime from previous work and then taken a step back to see how these systems apply to considerations for a larger system.

It is not hard to see why so much would be blocked from view on the *Backtrack,* when the same phenomenon takes place during an individual's present incarnation. As an individual increasingly withdraws *Awareness* from a particular channel, more and more automatic circuitry is generated with regards to its consideration and handling.

This is one of the things we explore in Route-2 and the similar developments of Route-3 using circuit-**flows**: inflows, out-flows and cross-flows—what they have been the *effect* of from others as *cause*; what they have *caused* to be an *effect* for others; and finally, what they've observed of another or others *causing* an *effect* on others.

All of this data is accumulated and stored on a particular channel—and that **slate** doesn't seem to *clear* between "*lives*." So, we are carrying a compounded accumulation of this and other *implanting* along the '*Spiritual Timeline.*' There is also an additional circuit that sometimes applies to systematic processing: what an individual has *caused* for themselves; which seems obvious but often requires the highest *Awareness* to confront directly, followed closely by what one has *out-flowed* to others, which we treated more specifically in Route-3E.

Sometimes, during *Beta-Defragmentation*, the "command lines" may occasionally target something for a *Seeker* where the answers or **concept** or *mental imagery* that results does not seem to "fit" with the present lifetime, this planet, or even this Universe. It might be easy to discount or invalidate the whole thing as some kind of "imaginative fantasy," but what we are most concerned with, from a technical standpoint, is whether or not the systematic processing produces positive gains for the *Seeker*. We do, however, want to avoid allowing the Mind-System to stir up too much false or fragmented information in the process of conducting light practice on the concept of the *Backtrack*. But mostly, we start with light exercises to simply start freeing up some attention-units for the *Backtrack*. So, Route-4A will be our initial *foray* on the *Backtrack*.

∆ ∆ ∆ ∆ ∆ ∆ ∆

Personal inclinations, preferences and interests in *this*

lifetime often stem from earlier on the *track*. Some may be related to certain *implanted* purposes and goals. Often these are "played out" or *"**dramatized**"* in thoughts and behavior based on what part of a particular goals-and-roles cycle an individual is currently playing at. Some of the roles and "personality **phases**" cycle back and forth. There are reoccurring **patterns** all down the *track* that seem universal to all of us, even though we each seem to be in a different part of it—or playing out a different part of it—in *this* lifetime.

We've all been around for a very long time and we have all played at each of the various roles and phases at one time or another. We have all been kings; have all had that experience. We've had our positions usurped at some point. We've experienced assassinations. When we got tired of that, and realizing that the temple district, for example, seemed to outlive the lifespan of the palace, we've all been high priests or priestesses. And then we've all experienced having our sanctuary sacked and the ruining of the vestal virgins and decided maybe next time to be a soldier, because now *that's* the thing to be to survive. And failing continuance that way at some point, we move on to something else, usually in some way in opposition to what we were just doing.

The same Mind-System that we defragment for clearer *recall* in *this* lifetime is what we are treating on the *Backtrack*. In view of that fact, there are some mechanisms that we are already familiar with that we benefit from considering as we move forward. For example, the Mind likes to "fill-in-the-blanks" a lot in the absence of a clear view. This is a basic psychological phenomenon that has been experimented with for a very long time. It becomes a major factor in consolidating an objective version of events when experienced by multiple individuals subjectively. Those involved with "crime solving" or "event recording" have run into this quite frequently.

Sometimes, in low-*Awareness* situations, a person may "reactively" see what is expected or believed rather than what *is*. And as more time goes on and additional fragmentation ensues, the viewable memory that is recalled can change; the facts as they actually are for us can be altered by other information. Just as a word of advice: it is only when we treat something *As-It-Is,* rather than how we think it might be or should be or someone else says it is, that real defragmentation occurs. This is important to remember so you can balance out some of the "wishful thinking" attached to remembering past-lives. There is a lot we didn't want to remember—and there is a lot of data and memory that gets altered, just so it is more acceptable to us; or is altered to better fit a different understanding—or, more accurately, a misunderstanding—for similar circumstances of a more recent (but related) incident.

The physical or apparent qualities of civilization and environmental conditions of existence are also quite cyclic. Before an *Alpha-Spirit* got tagged as "*earthbound,*" we experienced other lifetimes on Earth-like planets elsewhere. Cultural themes and creative aspects and visible styles have all reoccurred many times—on Earth and elsewhere. So, if someone recollects a vague sense of scenery or quick glance of something that resembles artistic depictions of, let's say, *Ancient Greece* or *Ancient Egypt*, it is also quite possible that its content is connected to, for example, a civilization 500,000 years ago on Earth—or even millions of years ago somewhere else. It could also be 1500 years ago in Europe or whatever, but greater certainty is generally expected as more entangled energy on a *Seeker's Backtrack* is untangled.

For our introduction, Route-4A is "**conceptual**"; it's not as concerned with accuracy and rightness or forcing anything into view. We also aren't wanting to push a *Seeker* into fully committing to any of the details that do come into view as being set-in-stone. An individual has been mistaken before about vague recall in *this* lifetime; the same can be expected to some degree down the line in *Alpha-Defragmentation* until everything gets lined up. The whole reason there is so much *occlusion* on the *Backtrack* is because of how entangled it actually is.

—*Imagine* taking motion picture film and crunching up bunches of it into little balls along the strip-line —that film is going to be quite difficult to view with clarity.

—Now, *Imagine* taking all the parts of all different films with scenes that are related to one another and superimposing them all together to form one cluster mass of *imprints*—including those "dubbed-in" that aren't even our own experiences—and you've got a general idea of the content suspended on the line by an *implant*.

Well, when we talk about **flattening** turbulent energy wave-patterns in Systemology, that's basically what we're handling. By the way, that isn't Route-4A that I was giving you there; I just want to increase everyone's reality a bit more on what this is really all about.

When you're handling the *Backtrack*, it is best to just make note of everything that presents itself without getting too fixed to any of the ideas and without invalidating any of your recall as "made-up" when you find inconsistencies or the logic doesn't add up. Especially early into this work, a *Seeker* is not expected to find vivid certainty on all the details, but there is generally something true underlying what is recalled. Not only do we tend to "fill-in-the-blanks" on what we have a vague *Awareness* of, you also might consider that efforts could have been made to distort or alter details, and not always initiated by ourselves. Even in *this* lifetime, we have no shortage of other individual's acting to determine, or at least influence, the nature of our perceptions and considerations. You don't have to accept all the data that comes up as perfectly accurate; but if the *recall* given is invalidated altogether, then whatever kernel of truth that was presented in it can also be lost. And again, we have to go beyond the traditional contemporary ideas in our culture about accepting the possibilities of carrying some stuff along with us into *this* life. For example, you got a guy and they're just obsessed with the Celtic Druids, right? And they start to think, well, just maybe they were a Druid in a past-life. And then their friend is all, no, no, you just like the Druids a lot so you *think...* Well, does anyone stop to ask *why* this person *has* a fixation on the Druids in the first place? What—just some incredible random assortment of things presented in *this* life that added up to that? Doesn't make sense.

And there's a flip side to this that we began to figure in Route-3E. This person might have even been a Roman Soldier that was responsible for personally executing many Druids and priestesses. They can't face up to or confront that level of responsibility and somehow the guilt transfers. So, they may retain a vague recall from the perspective of their victim, because the end of the channel they were on is too unpleasant to face *As-It-Is*. And guess what, the grass is always greener apparently for the other guy, because the reverse can also take place. The individual was on the *effect* end and was brutally tortured and murdered by the Romans and so transference makes it easier to hold onto thinking you were on the winning end of things. The perception of **conflict** flips. This is why amateurs in this line of work run into so many "Julius Caesars" and those famous types turning up and stuff like that: *transference.* They were powerful prominent individuals that imprinted strongly on their victims on a mass scale. So, there's no reason to get too caught up on such "identities" in history, because you may run across something like that.

△ △ △ △ △ △

The entry-level method we're adopting for Route-4A is based on a discourse left for us years ago by *Brother Keno* and developed for his own spiritual awakening regimen that parallels our defragmentation in Systemology. He reminds us that our time on *this* Earth has just been "a drop in the bucket" in comparison to the millions of lifetimes spent in this and other Universes. "Earth-like" experiences—the type of imagery, themes and constructs found in lifetimes on *this* Earth—have been with us for quite a while and reflect the type of recollections that a *Seeker* is more readily able to confront at first, rather than the more foreign—"alien"—settings. The "Earth-like" *imprints* are those that we tend to find most commonly in "restimulation" in day-to-day life living on planet Earth—so, this makes them more accessible for beginners.

Route-4A is not concerned with intensive defragmentation. We're starting with some basic recollection of positive or pleasant lifetimes and settings—particularly related to those that you are already familiar with or have interest in. Like what I said previously concerning the Celtic Druid example, we're looking at what your favorite period of history is, or perhaps a certain culture or civilization that you seem to have an innate sense of increased interest in. Route-4A does not only have to pertain to "earthbound" experiences either, if a *Seeker* has a high **affinity** for certain types of fantasy reflecting the "*Magic Universe*" or "*Magic Kingdom*"—or even other more science-fiction themes involving "*outer space*"—than work with that. Just take whatever presents itself, one lifetime at a time. Our esteemed Brother's notes goes on to instruct:

> "Once you have made a selection, discard all the details, especially famous names and events, and

concentrate instead on the general character of the civilization. And if some historical detail strikes you as wrong, then discard it in favor of what you feel is appropriate because you might actually be sensing something from long ago and far away rather than the recent Earth civilization that you have read about."

[*With familiar and pleasant lifetimes*] "...you can probably trust your feelings as to what kind of person you were and what kind of things you might have been doing. With a good lifetime, you do not have as much of a tendency to substitute pleasant experiences for the harsh ones that actually happened because the actual experiences *really were* pleasant.

"Now consider what kind of activity you might have enjoyed doing in such a civilization. Visualize an incident of doing this activity, trying to get the colors and sounds and any details that seem right. Adjust this based on what *feels* right or wrong until you are happy with it. Consider that it might be an approximation of a true recollection."

[*After doing this a few times with various activities*] "...look over the various occurrences and see if you can sort them into a sequence of which might have happened first and so forth. Consider what kind of job or station in life feels appropriate. Visualize incidents of performing the task in question. Sort these together with the other ones into a sort of time-line. It will help to write this down leaving much space for additions.

"Consider what kind of people you might have cared for in these circumstances; friends, lovers, parents, children... Try to visualize some really good incidents with these people and add them to the sequence. Consider if there might have been some really good event that might have happened;

some personal success or an important occurrence that affected your life favorably. Again visualize incidents and add them in." [*And just in case*] "...some bad thing occurs to you which you need to face, go ahead and" [*confront that*] "...and add it into the sequence of events. But balance it by spotting some of the good things again." [*In Route-4A we*] "...don't go charging off in search for the horrible things that happened..."

The point to Route-4A is to get some practice on making recollections and being able to document them for personal clarity; getting a whole sense of what that unique environment and lifetime consists of, in regards to our perception of it and having a reality on the type of scenery or sensation associated. The documentation is only a skeletal outline of the impressions that we receive; not something that we have to *stick to* or take as any absolute data. This type of exploration is incredibly effective in opening up new realizations on what is possible in the past. Its practice may also assist in directly untangling light fragmentation as well—much as the '*Creative Ability*' exercises from the "*Imaginomicon*" (*Liber-3D*) did.

Δ Δ Δ Δ Δ Δ Δ

Once you have a well-rounded account written down from the preliminary exercise, the next step for Route-4A includes the application of basic "Route-2" analytical recall, as given in the Grade-III handbook "*Crystal Clear*" (*Liber-2B*) or Grade-III "*Systemology Handbook*"—and, of course, we have reprinted that material in our complete 'Beta-Defrag' manual, the new "*Systemology-180*" book.

There are other applications of the earlier Routes; we experimented with all of them at the Systemology Society for Grade-V. But, our target is now obviously on past-life *imprints* and *implanting*, which is not how earlier routes were presented. So, in the spirit of progress, previous material selected specifically for past-life "roles and goals" is now summarized as "*Route-30*"—and this is also included in "*Systemology-180.*"

Route-30 represents the *minimum* of what is applied to "Class-4" *Piloting* of *Implants* and the *Backtrack*. This "*Grand Tour*" of earlier material essentially employs all of the basic Routes. It consists of the most basic *Processing Command Lines* (*PCLs*) from each main category. All of those additional systematic processing techniques described along with those categories in our earlier books are only utilized if the more direct route or PCL does not seem to be achieving changes that result in the improvement of the *Seeker* overall. A little bit of intuition goes a long way in being able to eliminate premature use of a PCL that contains wording that doesn't make sense for the application or the *Seeker*. They can often be reworded in some way. Inappropriate PCL wording only adds to a *Seeker's* confusion when really, they are trying to raise their certainty and *Awareness* to confront their past.

Although there are many applications, the original purpose of this "Route-30 Defragmentation Intensive" concerns *Implanting* on the *Backtrack*—which we will be more concerned with as we progress through Grade-V. But in brief, it means removing "charge" from "goals and roles" that are apparently programmed—*implanted* artificially; then dramatized and built upon during one's lifetime— and subsequently, many lifetimes. But this processing skeleton may be modified to fit the most appropriate wording to apply to some other type of "**terminal**" or targeted purpose as well. So, I'm sharing it here with you for the first time at this Spring 2023 conference with the instructions and PCLs exactly as it appears in the new "*Systemology-180*" book.

"Route-2" assists in increasing willingness to confront, but it also tends to take heat off the turbulence when a *Seeker* recalls positive aspects of the processing subject. By using multiple circuits, a *Seeker* is also able to analyze the goal or terminal from the outside, so to speak. PCLs are run alternately in series **repetitively**. They may be reworded as appropriate to the "terminal" used. As given here, they originally targeted an **archetypal** 'phase' or '**personality** role' as the "terminal"—one that represents a basic *implant* "to dramatize a goal."

RECALL being ___.

RECALL another person being ___.

RECALL others being ___.

As demonstrated in Grade-III, component factors of attention are tied to communication, reality agreements and the **degree** of "likingness" (liking, attraction) shared between an individual and a terminal or environmental aspect. This application of "Route-2" assists in accessing memory. The basic *facets* of each instance should also be *spotted*. If no event easily **resurfaces**, an "IMAGINE" PCL can be used.[*]

RECALL a time you were in good communication with a(n) ___.

RECALL a time a(n) ___ was in good communication with you.

RECALL a time another was in good communication with a(n) ___.

RECALL a time a(n) ___ was in good communication with another.

---

[*]   Only a few examples from each series were read out loud during the original lecture, but the complete PCL list is provided here exactly as given in the manuscript copies of the "*Systemology-180*" workbook issued at the Spring 2023 Systemology conference.

RECALL a time others were in good communication with a(n) ___.

RECALL a time when a(n) ___ was in good communication with others.

RECALL a time you agreed with a(n) ___.

RECALL a time a(n) ___ agreed with you.

RECALL a time another agreed with a(n) ___.

RECALL a time a(n) ___ agreed with another.

RECALL a time others agreed with a(n) ___.

RECALL a time when a(n) ___ agreed with others.

RECALL a time you felt you liked a(n) ___.

RECALL a time a(n) ___ liked you.

RECALL a time another felt they liked a(n) ___.

RECALL a time a(n) ___ liked another.

RECALL a time others felt they liked a(n) ___.

RECALL a time when a(n) ___ liked others.

Communication is indicative of a free flow of energy that can be exchanged. Breaks in communication lead to the development of *barriers*, automatically generated masses. Use "IMAGINE" techniques to conceive of a continuous out-flow of communication (speech) between terminals. With the running of each PCL, IMAGINE the largest out-pouring of speech possible. A PCL is run excessively until it begins to slow; then switch to the next one.

IMAGINE saying specific things to a(n) ___.

IMAGINE a(n) ___ saying specific things to you.

IMAGINE another saying specific things to a(n) ___.

IMAGINE a(n) ___ saying specific things to another.

IMAGINE others saying specific things to a(n) ___.

IMAGINE a(n) ___ saying specific things to others.

Part of an individual's break in communication, and other turbulence on a particular line, results from accumulated failures to **help** and assist others. Fragmentation results if the *Seeker* does not also balance the "failures" they hold on to with the memory of times when they are successful. On the *Backtrack*, a particular 'goal' and 'role' decays into the next one (usually an opposing one) after so much "failure" using a particular *personality-phase* has been calculated. If these cannot be *spotted* with 'RECALL', then use 'IMAGINE', as with the remainder of this Grand Tour.

RECALL a time you helped a(n) ___.

RECALL a time a(n) ___ helped you.

RECALL a time another helped a(n) ___.

RECALL a time a(n) ___ helped another.

RECALL a time others helped a(n) ___.

RECALL a time a(n) ___ helped others.

Another "**hot-button**" coinciding with *Help* is a failure to *Protect*. Such imprints are generally more intense and may even include violence. A *Seeker* runs into their stream of "losses" (including "love")—as well as matters of trust and betrayal. "Route-2" will not reduce emotional entanglement **associated** with "loss" and so the *Seeker* should focus on the other end of the **spectrum**.

RECALL a time you protected a(n) ___.

RECALL a time a(n) ___ protected you.

RECALL a time another protected a(n) ___.

RECALL a time a(n) ___ protected another.

RECALL a time others protected a(n) ___.

RECALL a time a(n) ___ protected others.

One of the issues with using a '*personality-phase*' or an implanted 'goal/role' to solve "problems" is that once this is done, an individual is likely to *calcify* that method of behavior (or thought or effort) and use it as an absolute for the handling of all difficulties. This leads to further problems, often of a greater magnitude. An individual is operating in such a way as to solve the problems that oppose the 'goals' they are fixed to.

When applied to unravel the *Backtrack*, a *Solo Pilot* will *spot* a particular problem (with the first PCL) and then as many solutions accessibly *spotted* afterward. Then another problem is selected as a target. As one *spots* earlier and earlier 'goal-problems' on the *Backtrack*, one realizes that "solutions" eventually lead to another "goal" on a 'chain' that was first implanted far back on the *Spiritual Timeline*.

a) -What problem might a(n) ___ have with another (or others)?

   -What solutions might a(n) ___ have to that problem?

b) -What problem might another (or others) have with a(n) ___?

   -What solutions might they have to that problem?

c) -What problem might a(n) ___ observe between others?

   -What solutions might a(n) ___ have to their problem?

d) -What problem might a(n) ___ create for themselves?

   -What solutions might a(n) ___ have to that problem?

"Route-3E" reveals that an individual does things and then hides them and withdraws reach and communication. It doesn't really matter what the original **intention** was; in the end, they begin to **hold-back** their action as Cause. It is important to rehabilitate realizations of being Cause and not just focus on more negative '**Harmful-Acts**'—although these do need to be handled. We are concerned with all *out-flow*; both those acts which have actually been performed and those which have been **Held-back**.

a) What might a(n) ___ do to another?

\ What might a(n) ___ hide from another?

b) What might another do to a(n) ___?

\ What might another hide from a(n) ___ ?

c) What might a(n) ___ do to others?

\ What might a(n) ___ hide from others?

d) What might a(n) ___ do to themselves?

\ What might a(n) ___ hide from themselves?

e) What might you do to a(n) ___?

\ What might you hide from a(n) ___?

Another *hot-button* for *processing* is *"change."* A *Seeker* that is resistant to change is also unwilling to improve. A compulsive **insistence** on change is no healthier. The '*Identity-Phases*' attached to "goal/roles" and problem-solving tend to be resistant to change (which is treated in Grade-IV).

a) What might a(n) ___ want to change in another?

\ What might a(n) ___ prevent changing in another?

b) What might another want to change in a(n) ___?

\ What might another prevent changing in a(n) ___ ?

c) What might a(n) ___ want to change in others?

\ What might a(n) ___ prevent changing in others?

d) What might a(n) ___ want to change in themselves?

\ What might a(n) ___ prevent changing in themselves?

e) What might you want to change in a(n) ___?

\ What might you prevent changing in a(n) ___?

Flows on a circuit are comprised of considerations toward communication, agreement and liking—all of which contribute to how an individual *understands* such-and-such. An upset occurs when these considerations are compulsively desired, forced, held-back and/or rejected. The most common PCLs for these combinations of *buttons* and *considerations* are listed here for *Backtrack* processing.

What communication might a(n) ___ inhibit in another?

What communication might another inhibit in a(n) ___?

What communication might a(n) ___ inhibit in others?

What communication might a(n) ___ hold-back from saying?

What communication might you inhibit a(n) ___ from saying?

What communication might a(n) ___ force on another?

What communication might another force on a(n) ___?

What communication might a(n) ___ force on others?

What communication might a(n) ___ force on themselves?

What communication might you force on a(n) ___?

What communication might a(n) ___ desire from another?

What communication might another desire from a(n) ___?

What communication might a(n) ___ desire from others?

What communication might a(n) ___ make themselves desire?

What communication might you desire from a(n) ___?

What agreement might a(n) ___ reject from another?

What agreement might another reject from a(n) ___?

What agreement might a(n) ___ reject from others?

What agreement might a(n) ___ make themselves reject?

What agreement might you reject from a(n) ___?

What agreement might a(n) ___ force on another?

What agreement might another force on a(n) ___?

What agreement might a(n) ___ force on others?

What agreement might a(n) ___ force on themselves?

What agreement might you force on a(n) ___?

What agreement might a(n) ___ desire from another?

What agreement might another desire from a(n) ___?

What agreement might a(n) ___ desire from others?

What agreement might a(n) ___ make themselves desire?

What agreement might you desire from a(n) ___?

What might a(n) ___ inhibit another from liking?

What might another inhibit a(n) ___ from liking?

What might a(n) ___ inhibit others from liking?

What might a(n) ___ hold-back themselves from liking?

What might you inhibit a(n) ___ from liking?

What might a(n) ___ force another to like?

What might another force a(n) ___ to like?

What might a(n) ___ force others to like?

What might a(n) ___ force themselves to like?

What might you force a(n) ___ to like?

What might a(n) ___ desire another to like?

What might another desire a(n) ___ to like?

What might a(n) ___ desire others to like?

What might a(n) ___ make themselves desire to like?

What might you desire a(n) ___ to like?

By following game-conditions "TO SURVIVE" in *Beta-Existence*, an individual allows themselves to commit "Hostile-Acts"—which are then buried under layers of justification. Once an action is *spotted* (in the first PCL), many answers can be given in response to justification. When the first pair are *flattened*, move to the second. When there are no more answers for the pair, run it again for new responses.

a) What would a(n) ___ do to ensure their own survival?

\ What justifications would they have for that?

b) What would a(n) ___ stop others from doing to ensure their own survival?

\ What justifications would they have for that?

A *Seeker's* primary justification computation or justification imprint is generally attached to the implanted "goal/ role." In a nutshell the processing determines what an individual uses (as a consideration) to justify themselves as right and make others wrong—as stated in the PCLs.

How might a(n) ___ make themselves right?

How might a(n) ___ make others wrong?

In order to check-out that there is no significant charge on a channel remaining after the Grand Tour, the following is a "Route-0" communication process that may even allow a *Seeker* to experience "**Zu-Vision**" as an *End-Point*. This is not the absolute purpose of the defragmentation, but may ensue as a result. If this Grand Tour has not fully defragmented the channel (or implant or goal, &tc.), at least the bulk of the turbulence and fragmentation will have been lifted off of the line, allowing for enough *Actualized Awareness* to approach other systematic processing techniques. An experienced *Pilot* knows the ultimate realization of this technique already,‡ but it should still be answered within the rules of handling systematic processing sessions.

From where could you communicate to a(n) ___?

From where could a(n) ___ communicate to you?

From where could a(n) ___ communicate to others?

From where could a(n) ___ communicate to themselves?

---

‡ The supreme realization is that anything can communicate with anything from anywhere. But individual locations should be *spotted* to assist in "grounding" a *Seeker* at the end of the Intensive.

.: LECTURE FIVE :.
HANDLING IMPRINTS ON THE BACKTRACK
("ROUTE-4B" & "ROUTE-1R")
18, MARCH 2023

Quite often during systematic processing or personal meditations with the training, a *Seeker* comes up with the idea of being "*stuck*" 'somewhere' on the *Backtrack*—and we started running into this phenomenon at the Systemology Society from the very beginning, even in the treatment of this present incarnation. Of course, in terms of *actual* space-time "location," we know from our upper-level philosophy that the *Alpha-Spirit* is not actually located in *this* Universe and has not moved from its static position at "7.0" on our Standard Model. Only considerations attaching an association to identify with an *organic-body* allow it to be locatable in *this time-space.* Only its considerations for *reality* and a *Universe* have carried its agreeable or acceptable range of **viewpoints** down the line. This, of course, gives the illusion of time and space based on the ordering and sequence of our experience—and thus a *track* to represent this perception of a '*Spiritual Timeline*'.

So, while an *Eternal Spirit*, back behind all this, essentially *Is*, it has the spiritual ability to superimpose layers of postulates and considerations upon what it is in agreement with concerning *reality*. And, although we have, in the end, agreed to accept this, most certainly there have been many *impositions* from outside—*other-determined*—sources that have affected or influenced the considerations we carry. And some of this is just inherent in the systemology of "*Shared Universes*" that we take up more in Grade-VI; some of it is not intended to be malicious from the start. It simply started with agreements between *Alpha-Spirits* concerning **parameters** of "sharing" experience of the same "Universe" in which to play a *game*. We are, in some respects, still operating under *those* parameters, plus however many more have since been added or *implanted*, for us to be operating the viewpoint of a *genetic-vehicle* in *this* Universe.

What is it, then, that is *sticking* along the way? It would probably be better considered that an individual is having things *stick onto them* along the perceived sequence of the time-line, rather than that they are being **inhibited** from motion somewhere down the way. But to keep with the semantic vocabulary more common to the Human Condition: what is *stuck* along the *track* is an individual's *Attention*—the 'Attention-Units' or 'Awareness Units' of *Zu*, the 'Spiritual Awareness' that *is* the individual, representative of the *Alpha-Spirit's* creations and interactions as experience.

As the **continuity** or zero-point of a *Beta-Existence* has descended, relatively speaking, with the condensation and solidification of Universes, so too have the considerations maintained by the *Alpha-Spirit* along the way. In fact, we have reason to believe in our Metaphysical Systemology, that the two are the same, or at least codependent: that *this* Universe maintains a certain solidity in line with the solidity and energy-mass that has been fed into it. This is what makes the esoteric "Gate" phenomenon possible; at each level of *ascent*, the *threshold* is defined by a certain *screen* or level of *filtering*—kind of like, where nothing larger than "such-and-such" an energy-mass could pass through at each stage.

We have already differentiated between the old religious idea of *having* a "soul" from the New Thought concept of the actual *Self* or "I-AM" *being* the "soul" or "spirit." For our purposes here, *that* actual state is safe or eternally remote or untouchable—except by relative considerations, of course—so the real spiritual "battle going on" concerning us, is really the "Mind-System" that is being carried along the *track*. Because, it is the *only* "thing" that is consistently picking up and accumulating mass that we consider ourselves to *have* along the way—and it is the very thing that gives us this sense of "time" on the *Backtrack* in the first place. Therefore, let us return the proper understanding the Greeks had for the "soul"—which is the *psyche*—and consider that the entrapment of our descent is in regard to the Mind: the *imprints* and *implants*; the *postulates* and *considerations*; this is what we must defragment in order to ascend through these Gateways toward Infinity.

The first thing to know about the Mind is that you *can know* about the Mind. The aura of 'mystery' that enshrouds the Mind is, quite frankly, *implanted* so someone doesn't become *Self-Aware* and "break" the *game*. So, you should not, now at this point of Class-4 Piloting, be very hesitant to handle the Mind directly. Of course, it is important that we actually have the training and techniques to properly handle the Mind—to handle the imprinting that seems blocked from our view—before we just start rampantly charging in and stirring up things that we aren't prepared to confront. The unwillingness or uncertainty to handle or confront is part of what shields our view; so, this is handled systematically based on its effectiveness in practice and not simply a series of arbitrary rules we came up with just to seem cryptic or have a bunch of esoteric levels and grades.

The next component of the Mind-System to understand is that it is made up of *impressions* or *imprints* that are a mental record of events, incidents, perceptions and associations—all of which are used to formulate a particular "package" used for considering and interacting as experience. When considering our Standard Model, all of these operate below the level of **Alpha-Thought** because the Mind-System in which they operate has already been *postulated* into existence as a mechanism for their storage

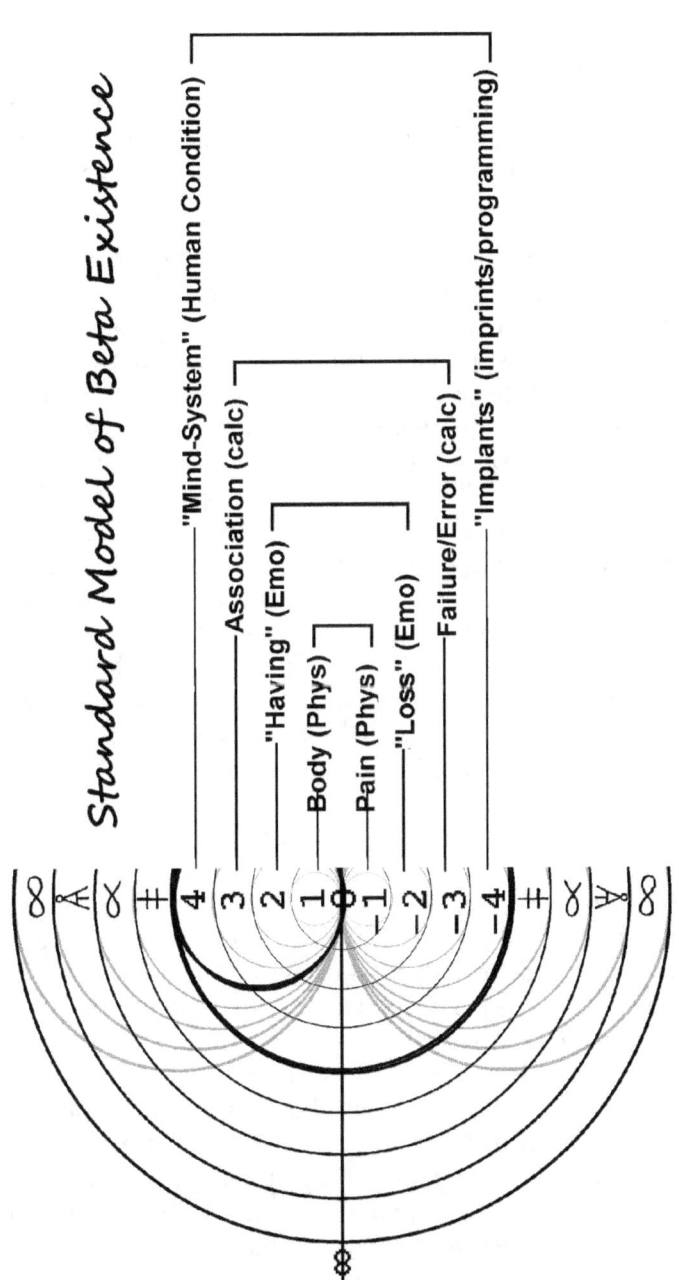

Standard Model of Beta Existence

—"Mind-System" (Human Condition)

—Association (calc)

—"Having" (Emo)

—Body (Phys)

—Pain (Phys)

—"Loss" (Emo)

—Failure/Error (calc)

—"Implants" (imprints/programming)

and handling. This is the true nature of the auto-mated-machinery that we introduce to a *Seeker* in the "*Imaginomicon*" (*Liber-3D*). The Mind-System is that inter-mediary between *Self* and its experience of any *Beta-Exist-ence*—and as *it* has developed mass, so have the consider-ations of *Beta-Existence*.

At the material level of *this* Universe, the type and qual-ity of energetic-mass we are talking about would seem insignificant or irrelevant; and in fact, only some of the most high-sensitivity precision instruments in this world seem to register any of its effects, and even then, only when it is in restimulation or actively impinging on the individual's reality. This is what you tend to find when using *GSR-Biofeedback metering* to assist Alpha-Defrag-mentation for the *Backtrack*. But we aren't just concerned with what's **negligible** for *this* world, so what our GSR ex-periments essentially confirmed is that there is a meta-psychological and spiritual component to these energet-ic-masses. The alleviation or release of entangled energy on this 'Spiritual Timeline' is **one-to-one** with the concept we have always held in our Mardukite and Sys-temology work for a 'Pathway to Ascension'.

△ △ △ △ △ △

Route-4B is the application of R1-R for the *Backtrack*. Cer-tainly there are some differences in the approach; but if you have practiced "Route-1 Revised" in the newer edi-tion of *Liber-One*, "*Tablets of Destiny (Revelation)*"—or its in-clusion in "*Systemology-180*"—then you'll already have a handle on this. It just requires the inclusion of considera-tions for the *Backtrack* as I've been describing. When ap-plied to the *Backtrack* with a GSR-Meter, its inclusion is integral to the more formal Alpha-Defragmentation pro-cedure we refer to as Route-4G. So, all of this information is taken into account as we continue progressing along the *Pathway*; only our understanding of its application increases with each *Class* of *Piloting*. But it is expected that a *Pilot* or *Seeker* is retaining this knowledge along the way—for training purposes—so that we are not consistently having to recover the same territory of instruction along the way.

We again find us in the realm of handling *imprints*—which means we have not strayed far from the original purposes behind a practical development of systematic processing for our philosophy. However, we are concerned now with the *imprinting incidents* that are connected onto strings or chains from the experiences of an incarnation or lifetime previous to this one. Most often it begins with an event or experience in *this* one; and this is what 'triggers' or 'restimulates' the energetic-mass of the *imprinting* in the form of a '**mental image**' or artificial playback of stored and associated information. Even if this is not experienced in the present moment as a "holographic" '*mental image*', it is this form of data-collection and handling that is still taking place. The individual does not have to have the *Awareness* to experience a precision "replay" of all that data in order for the accumulated considerations and automated-mechanisms to have an effect. The Mind-System is geared and wired to have much more immediate responses than that.

What have we learned about *imprints* and *incidents* in all of these years? We know that in addition to biological unconsciousness, *imprinting incidents* include perceptions of extreme unpleasantness, pain and loss. When we talk about "reach and withdrawal" in Grade-III, we note that an individual often '*flinches*' or '*withdraws*' away from painful and unpleasant incidents. Since they are unwilling to confront the content of the information contained in the incident, the individual will develop additional unpleasant and often irrational associations between the *facets* connected to it. The degradation of the individual as an *Alpha-Spirit* occurs when considerations of unwillingness to confront the things connected with the incident begin to affect that which the individual is willing to be, do or have. Thus their considerations for acceptable existences and viewpoints decline.

In Grade-IV, we realized that the same phenomenon was integrally connected to the Mind-System. In the "*Imaginomicon*" (*Liber-3D*), we began to examine more closely at that which the *Seeker* is unwilling to be, do, or have anymore; well, at first it happens on a selective level, but quickly becomes automatic. The automated mechanisms and reactive mental machinery all maintain their creation from the *Alpha-Spirit's* own energy. Who else would be maintaining the individual Mind-System along the entire 'Spiritual Continuum'? Assigning source doesn't get us out of the woods entirely. Too often, an *Alpha-Spirit* eventually loses control of their own mental machinery altogether—and this is where the concept of the "subconscious" developed in more contemporary forms of understanding.

An *Alpha-Spirit* can retain the *Knowingness* of its experience without compulsively creating energetic masses along their '*Spiritual Timeline*'. Those '*mental images*' that are knowingly created and dispersed consciously at will are not what is turbulently stored on the *Backtrack*. Fragmentation is that which divides an *Alpha-Spirit's* creative ability or *Awareness* in a way that makes the individual more "solid"—which for our purposes, is to say, "lower" on the *Beta-Awareness Scale* or a "lower fixed viewpoint" on the Standard Model. Being reduced in *Awareness* and uncertain of its near-infinite ability to create for itself, the *Alpha-Spirit* developed the Mind-System to essentially *copy* a *facsimile* of the experience. But then the same mechanisms were also eventually used maliciously against the individual to trap them.

The *unconfronted* past is what contributes the greatest to our fragmentation. All of the incidents lock up on top of each other and develop the energetic-mass that weighs us down to lower *Beta-Existences*. And it is what we do not *confront*—what we do not come around the front of to face *As-It-Is*—that we seem to carry with us on our *track*, because it is that which we are never rid of. It is those *traps* and *pitfalls* that we seem to find ourselves in time and time again. The same reactive mechanisms we once put into play to assist us in handling dangers, so we could focus on something else, have eventually been turned against us. The resolution only comes from handling it. When we run, it gives chase. When we push against it, it becomes more solid. When we try to pretend it is something it is not, it only persists. And, of course, this has been going on for us for a very long time.

Details concerning the *"Reactive Control Center"* (RCC) of the Mind-System—the relatively lowest order of circuitry in the Mind-System—are treated in depth in *"The Tablets of Destiny (Revelation)"* (*Liber-One*). We also first defined what an *imprint* and *imprinting incident* is during that initial phase of Grade-III. So, when the circumstances of daily-life "stir up" or "trigger" the *imprint*, we say that it is *restimulated*. And this only results from the stuff that remains *unconfronted*. Depending on the level of *Awareness* maintained in the present, or the amount of *other-determinism* inherent in the *imprint*, the individual tends to bring the content of the *imprint* into the present moment and experiences not only the unpleasant sensations but the associated considerations as well. Naturally, this lowers our **Self-determinism** and *Actualized Awareness*.

One of the key realizations necessary for a *Seeker* to achieve from *Grade-IV Beta-Defragmentation*—a prerequisite to the Wizard Grade work, you might say—is that an individual themselves, the *Alpha-Spirit*, is the one that is creating the 'mental states' and 'mental machinery' that stores and then inflates the **dead-memory** of painful experience. At this juncture of the standard-issue Human Condition, much of this is operating compulsively and in a state of *unknowingness* (or '*subconscious*', if you prefer), but it may still be brought back under the proper control of *Self*—the one who is creating it in the first place. Since they are not confronted they are automatically generated as reminders, which may have originally served to some beneficial gain to the *Alpha-Spirit* early on its *track,* but which has since become detrimental to its continuance at the highest ideal states of *Knowingness* and *Beingness.*

When an individual doesn't face something *As-It-Is*, there is a lack of true information or *Awareness* for that area. Yet, whatever it is, the individual doesn't want it to happen again. So, while it is not *confronted As-It-Is*, the individual doesn't want to consciously remember it, but is also afraid to some extent to forget it altogether. To resolve this issue, an *imprint* or *impression* is made of the incident—a '*mental image*' or '*facsimile copy*' of a picture stored in the Mind-System—that allows for associations and reactive-mechanisms that an individual doesn't actually have to look at or control to have an effect.

While the solution is simple, the application in practice as systematic processing seems to elude some *Seekers* that have studied these same mechanisms at earlier Grades. But, as we addressed in Grade-III, raising the willingness to confront the content of these old incidents also increased an individual's *Actualized Awareness.* By analyzing and confronting the content of the Mind-System with high-level *Awareness*, a *Seeker* regains control over the mechanisms that cause the reactivity and entanglement of mental circuits. Defragmentation means to rise above and operate beyond the influence of the Mind-System.

Δ Δ Δ Δ Δ Δ

The basic instructions for Route-4B are quite simple to

apply—just as we found with Route-4A. A *Seeker* should be in the practice of making a written record of their processing session when *Flying-Solo*. Should a *Seeker* choose to work with a *Co-Pilot*, this is something that would also make that more efficient; but again, all of the systematic processing can be practiced by a solitary *Seeker*, so long as it is still *Piloted* correctly. A *Seeker* or *Pilot* should also review the details and instruction regarding Route-1 (or R-1R) before applying the same fundamental theory to Route-4B. With all this is mind, the basic steps of Route-4B are as follows:—

Firstly, there is the matter of locating an incident—particularly an *imprinting incident*, but this can be practiced with anything, even as simple as the incident of first walking in *that door* this afternoon. An incident like that does not likely have any real turbulence associated with it, thus you wouldn't get in any trouble by mishandling it in early practice. There isn't really a great concern for mishandling at all if a *Seeker* or *Pilot* has been adequately trained and practiced in the use of the techniques and exercises.

The next step is to *spot* or determine *when* the incident occurred. With this, you may have to be a bit intuitive when applying it to "past-life" events. If you think it was between 40 and 50 years ago, do your best to zero-in on it. See if it feels like it was *more than* or *less than* 45 years ago. This is where a GSR-Meter can really come in handy; but the meter in Route-4G is really only displaying a reaction objectively to what is happening with a *Seeker* subjectively. The same answers could be intuited and determined without any such instrumentation, but for efficiency and practice, they can certainly be of effective assistance.

Determining the *timing* of an incident is critical to locating it—or "contacting" it—on the *Backtrack*. One of the purposes of the earlier Route-4A procedure is to get into practice with ordering the sequence of events in relation to other events across a long span of perceived 'time'. This, of course, leads us right into our third step of *spotting* or determining the *duration* of the incident, meaning "how long" it took place, or "how much" time it took to happen. Having a sense of the "time-span" assists in recall during processing and other recollections later.

Then, once the matter of *time* has been spotted, the next phase concerns *locating* the incident in *space*. And we mean this exactly as it sounds: the "where" of the incident. You might get a sense of the basic direction from where your present viewpoint is— and perhaps distance. See if you can get a sense of this intuitively (or with a GSR-Meter) after handling the *timing*. Keep in mind, it is sometimes inaccurate to simply locate something on the *Backtrack* just based on visual cues alone. We cannot assume, for example, that the architectural style depicted in our more recent history on Earth is the only manifestation of this type.

Just as we handled a duration of time that is located on the *line*, the next part of the *spatial* phase is to *spot* or determine the actual "size" of the incident—meaning the amount of space that it occupied. For example, was it within a room or chamber indoors, or did it cover a range of miles while traveling, or however this may apply. We can only really provide a basic set of instruction on such matters that will cover all examples when it is applied in an actual systematic processing session.

These preliminary steps all assist in "contacting" the energy that is entangled on the *Backtrack* in regards to an *imprinting incident,* or in practice, with any incident that we have experienced. Just as in Route-1, once the incident is contacted, then the *Seeker* "moves" to the actual time when the incident occurred. Normally, **cathartic-processing** from Route-1 is not presented as a *Solo* exercise, but in this case, we qualify a *Class-4* trainee to do so, this far along the *Pathway.* So, try to "mentally" recreate the *facets* of the incident around you, as if you were actually there. Note as many of the perceptions or details as you can.

Then, move through the incident—do your best to re-experience, and of course, *confront,* everything you find in the incident; then, finally, open your eyes and write it all down. Since there is no two-way communication in *Solo-Piloting,* the "writing-down" phase is critical in getting "separate" from the incident and its turbulent charge in present-time. A *Seeker* would then "move" to the beginning of the incident and go through it again, noting down the details each time—and doing this as many times as is necessary to, as we say in Systemology, *"process-out"* the fragmentation.

During Grade-IV research and development concerning "mental imagery" we discovered more about *imprints;* enough to cause us to even revise our original processing routine. But specifically, when dealing with *imprints* in this "confront it *As-It-Is"* method, one of two different things will generally occur during processing: either the entangled energy will *process-out* and the turbulence will desensitize, therefore causing the intensity of the "mental imagery" to soften; or else there will be an accumulation of entangled energy from *earlier* on the *Backtrack* that keeps the turbulence from *flattening* and thus makes the experience of the "mental imagery" seem more solid.

In early *Solo* practices, similar to what we found in Route-1, if the imprinting incident is *processing-out,* then each time a *Seeker* moves through it, new *facets* should *resurface* that may not have been noticed on a previous run. Or else, sometimes, the details seem to rearrange themselves into a more accurate sequence—and above all, the *Seeker* should be experiencing some sense of "release" or "relief" in being able to increase their level of *confront* with certainty. If, however, the *imprint* seems to feel more solid or the *incident* becomes more difficult to run with each pass, then there is likely something *earlier* underlying it. This may be an earlier incident on the timeline, or it may be that the *timing* or *duration* that you originally determined about the incident is not fully accurate. So, with the new information in tow, you then can look to see if *this* incident had an earlier start, rather than the point that you have been "moving" through from.

When the *imprint* becomes harder to *process,* and there is no earlier beginning to it, then what you are dealing with is the restimulation of an even *earlier imprinting-incident.* This might still be from *this* lifetime or it may start leading a *Seeker* directly into "past-lives" on the *Backtrack.* It is also possible that there is both an earlier *imprinting-incident* in *this* lifetime, as well as, an even earlier *imprinting-incident* from "past-lives" on the *Backtrack.* In this case, the *Seeker* may be required to confront the earlier current-life incident before the recollections from the even earlier "past-life" incident will come into view. There is no strict criteria beyond this that applies to all *Seekers*; we have all had different events and sequences of events impinge upon our 'Spiritual Timeline' for a very long time, and so there will be certain *facets* of life that require more intensive defragmentation for one individual than another. The basic principles apply across the board, but at Grade-V, their application requires a bit of intuition to get the full desired results from the techniques and exercises.

Δ Δ Δ Δ Δ Δ Δ

In terms of "past-life" exploratory research, once a *Seeker* has confronted the nature of an experience in *this* life and desensitized any associated turbulence that is accessible, then they are certainly free to be willing to confront earlier similar aspects on the *Backtrack*. But it is unwise for *Seekers* that are still getting practice on how to handle these energetic-masses during *Beta-Defragmentation* in the earlier Grades to go "in search of" a lot of turbulent memory without the willingness, and therefore ability, to confront it. Another factor that affects the clarity and handling is that the amount of turbulent *"charge"* on the *line* is inherently proportional to the amount of literal *fragmentation* and *distortion* of the data.

This means the more heavily *implanted imprints* and most serious *incidents* will have the most 'mystery' and 'falsehood' enshrouding them—and thus we want to consistently improve a *Seeker's* creative ability, *Actualized Awareness* and 'spiritual horsepower', to effectively increase the degree or level of fragmentation that an individual is **capable** and willing to handle. While the whole process or progress on the *Pathway* toward the goals we have fixed for Grade-V may seem tedious or redundant from early on in Systemology, as a *Seeker* improves and increases in the areas I've mentioned, they are able to handle more sweeping areas of the *Backtrack*—its *implants* and *programming*—with higher powered *Awareness* in shorter periods of processing session time.

So, with Route-4B, when you decide that there is an earlier beginning or an earlier incident, then you start from the beginning of the preliminary steps with the *dating* and *locating*—making sure to write down all the details of the new earlier incident. And then for each "move" through, you simply work through from the beginning of the incident and "run" it to the end; of which you will likely have to "move" through the incident multiple times. Make sure to write the details down about each of the earlier beginnings or incidents that are contacted on the "chain." This will help in better orienting and sequencing other data on the *Backtrack* as well. Any systematic practice in handling the data on the *Backtrack* is beneficial to a *Seeker* at the Wizard Grades.

The '*End-Point*' for processing a singular *imprinting-incident* or "chain" is, of course, the "release" or "relief" for the individual, at least concerning *facets* of that particular "channel" or "terminal." In Route-1, this systematic regimen is referred to as "*resurfacing* and *reduction*"—and the same principle applies here. Others have considered the processing phenomenon as a "discharge" of energetic turbulence along a circuit or channel; and then, of course, there is our original metaphysical thesis for Systemology concerning the *flattening* of a **wave-form** that has **collapsed** from potential into solidity. Regardless of the semantic **paradigm** applied to this, we are dealing with the same phenomenon of defragmentation.

Another indication of an 'End-Point' for one incident in Route-4B is the increased *Actualized Awareness* or new '*realizations*' in that area, or regarding that particular terminal, and so forth. Usually, fragmented considerations and viewpoints are generally "fixed" outside one's own full free *Self-determinism*. So, as one has freed up the circulation of energy on these circuits or 'mental paths' of association, the individual is much more likely to think more freely and clearly along those lines. The individual doesn't *have to* consider *anything* along those lines again, if they so wish; but of course, again, there is no inhibition or unwillingness to face or confront anything there either. That is the state of true defragmentation we are headed toward with the Wizard-Level work—and with the *Backtrack.*

These systematic "Routes" are meant to improve an individual's own inherent spiritual ability and *Awareness* as the *Alpha-Spirit*—and are systematic assistants to these ends. Ideally, an individual will reach a point of high-level, high-power, personal **Actualization** where the ability to confront existence *As-It-Is* will be sufficient in untangling the turbulent charge on any *line.* But, as we work our way up to this point, we continue to apply the gradient steps of exercises and techniques that incrementally progress our *Knowingness* and *Beingness* closer to its original and more ideal spiritual state. We have found that confronting the past and handling the *Backtrack* is the critical step at this juncture of our Ascension—and it is high time that we face it and reclaim the spiritual power that is ours.

.: LECTURE SIX :.
IMPLANTS ON THE BACKTRACK
("ROUTE-4V" & "ROUTE-4C")
19, MARCH 2023

Upper-level goals distinguishing our Wizard Level-1 systematic processing techniques and exercises are divided into four categories and are used sequentially in this order as a progressive routine or regimen toward high-power *Alpha-Defragmentation.* Many assumed that the presentation of the existence of the *Backtrack* is the only differentiation between Grade-V and our previously given aspects of Systemology. But, in combination with the *Backtrack,* we also have:

1.) Increasing the Actualized Awareness and Spiritual Power of the *Seeker.*
2.) Identifying the nature of an *Implant* and corresponding *Imprints.*
3.) Confronting the existence of *Implanting "As-It-Is"* to reclaim control.
4.) Elimination of the particular *Implanting* "platform" altogether.

Naturally, there will be some minute upper-level aspects that still probably won't be adequately handled for all cases until additional *Alpha-Defragmentation* research work is done later in Grade-VI; but the amount of *"charge"* taken off an individual's fragmented 'Spiritual Timeline' using Grade-V techniques will certainly assist any additional processing work a *Seeker* applies later along the *Pathway.* We must, at the very least, defragment an individual to a certain elevated level of *knowingness* and *realization* at Grade-V for any higher gradient of application to be reached. This is essentially the progressive gradient path we have been on since the start; because all along the way we have been incrementally *destimulating* the channels in order to increase *Actualized*

Awareness enough to go back and eradicate the automated-mechanisms and reactive-machinery of the Mind-System that have run out of our control.

*But, as my intent *here* is to get through the basic concepts and introduce the technicalities behind *all* of "Route-4"—except for Route-4G—at this conference, we had better keep pressing ahead, now that we have reached the last day.

Route-4C includes an exploration into the "roles and goals" *implanting* that takes place during the span of a 'Spiritual Timeline'. The concept and existence of *implants* became apparent early in our Systemology work—but their handling requires a *Seeker* having progressed to a point on the *Pathway* where their *Actualized Awareness* is high enough to confront their existence. We are, of course, dealing with what is esoterically described as the *Fifth Gate*, pertaining to "Mars"—having crossed the threshold of the "Sun" in Grade-IV; and "Venus" in Grade-III. Each of these steps has represented a certain layer of fragmentation, programming and encoding.

And while we have approached the gradients *systematically* rather than in the shadows of a *cultural mythos*, we are still treating the same *"Ladder of Lights"* phenomenon that was first revealed in the earliest Mardukite work regarding Mesopotamia. **Ancient Mystery Schools** treated the subject of "between-lives" *implanting* of the Human Condition and their own version of the *Backtrack* in order to cross the threshold of the *Fifth Gate*. For thousands of years, the Grade-IV and Grade-V methodology has been a "pass-not" barrier represented by a '*Wall of Fire*', in which those afflicted by the **assumption** of the standard-issue Human programming would be *implanted* to not approach; to fear their own immortality should they pass through.

---

* There is a break here in the original audio recording of this lecture.

But, so long as we are freed from our weights and chains to *this* world, we have nothing to fear in hastening our way through what is discovered to be a quite thin screen of flames. But, we must have a certainty on our own true immortality—and our existence as a *Spiritual Awareness Unit* or *Alpha-Spirit*—independent of *this* Universe and *these* bodies. Otherwise there is an incredible resistance inherent in seeking to break free of the heavy 'earth-bound' gravity systems. And "Mars"—this tier we are approaching on the *Pathway*—represents an influential screen of *implanting* and a '*spiritual force-field*', the likes of which has not yet been confronted in the former Routes and Grades of our Systemology.

Δ Δ Δ Δ Δ Δ

Before breaking into the nature of *implanting*, there are some preliminary exercises that we will disclose for this portion of the *Piloting* training—and these are aimed directly at the increase of *Actualized Awareness* prior to undertaking Route-4C (or its GSR-Metered application to Route-4G). These are objective exercises for increasing "presence" prior to "Route-4" and upper-level work. The regimen is not intended as an unlimited activity—such as with the "*Creative Ability Training*" in Grade-IV—but simply as a "defrag-booster" as a Grade-IV *Seeker* crosses over to applying the Grade-V methodology. It, however, directly builds upon the work presented in the "*Imaginomicon*" (*Liber-3D*). This new checkpoint is classified as Route-4V. Route-4V is applied *after* a *Seeker* has reality on the *Backtrack*, but *before* any work is done directly on "*Goals*" and *Implants*. You may use it prior to this point, but no stable *realizations* occur until a *Seeker* has perceived the *Backtrack*, even if only vaguely.

On all levels—and particularly in our *Metaspiritual Systemology*—we are very much concerned with the systematic **identification** and understanding of "Source" or "sources" as they apply to all systems. By a *source*, we mean that which is the creator or controller of some system; and these include the systems of *Reality* and what we experience as *Existence*—primarily *Beta-Existence*. The ability to concisely *spot a source* is critical to understanding from what point the control—a *start, stop* or *alteration*—of some system or creation has occurred. While this seems like trite philosophy, on a level of *Awareness* or *knowingness*, it is a key factor in the ability to confront something—a terminal, incident or even an *implant*—and to be able to confront it *As-It-Is*.

So, as a basic exercise, a *Seeker* should select some aspect —a situation or condition—and apply these two PCLs in alternation. This should be first practiced with light terminals or conditions that are not heavily charged or turbulent prior to being used as a method for intensive defragmentation.

SPOT something that might be a source for ___.

SPOT something that is probably not a source for ___.

Run those PCLs until there really aren't any more answers readily coming off for a particular aspect, and then apply it again to another one. And by "*Spot*," we do not necessarily mean that which is physically present in the room or physical environment, but rather to focus attention and *Awareness* on something, including what is on the *Backtrack*. The "end-point" *realizations* intended for these exercises are not necessarily pertaining to any specific "terminal" or condition, but rather to the understanding of "*Sources*" as a whole. An alternate 'New Thought' version of this same technique is:

SPOT a source.
  \ Notice something about it.

SPOT a no-source.†

---

† An additional researched example reads: "*non-source.*"

\ Notice something about it.

But that might be a bit esoteric for some *Seekers*. A *Pilot* could append the "notice something about it" to the first example; that would be okay, possibly even preferable for both solitary *Seekers* and to maintain two-way communication in *Co-Piloting*. Ultimately, these PCLs target considerations for *Beingness*. A *Pilot* wants to be aware of the entanglement of considerations present in a case that either does not identify anything as a source for anything, or that believes themselves to be the *only* source for everything—and thereby unwilling to grant *Beingness* to others. Either type of fragmentation is a major hindrance to further advancement on the *Pathway*. Chances are quite good that if the new *realizations* are not reached with these exercises, then the *Seeker* has not fully completed their *Beta-Defragmentation* regimen. If, however a *Seeker* is not hung up on these aspects, they are likely fine to continue on with the work.

Both states of extreme fragmentation revealed with Route-4V must be resolved for Grade-V. On the one hand: an individual that cannot identify *Sources* is still **misappropriating** cause for reality and existence. This individual may still be very hung up on the type of 'Mysticism' and 'Magic' explored in Grade-I. They remain constantly at the effect end of misunderstood phenomenon at every turn—the victim of a thousand non-existent hauntings and poltergeists in addition to anything that might actually be present. On the other hand: an individual that *only* identifies themselves as the *Source of All*— and nothing and no one else—is living in a grand delusion of '*meta-megalomania*'.

Now, let's consider *existence* and *creation*. When we talk about *reality* and the control over the experience of *existence*, we are also talking about *creation* and what *Is*—with a capital "*I*." We use that expression a lot in Systemology: "*As-It-Is*"; "*As-It-Is*." But some *Seekers* don't really have an appreciation for what is meant by that. So, for handling some "objective-style" PCLs, we start with focusing a *Seeker's* attention on a small object or a section of wall and run these conceptual PCLs in alternation: 1,2,3; 1,2,3.

1. Get the concept[‡] that you are creating it.

2. Get the concept that others are creating it.

3. Get the concept that nobody is presently creating it.

Once the *Seeker* has a sense of increased *Awareness*, the same exercise can be applied to another small object or another part of the wall, and so forth. Here, we would like to see an increased reality on the first circuit-flow in the PCLs: that *Self* is creating. In either case, this is followed up with a more "subjective-style" version that is intended to give a *Seeker* the sense of increased *Presence*. So, combined, we have a Wizard Grade version of increasing a *Seeker's* "presence" and "Awareness" in a systematic processing session that is akin to the standard practices used in all Grade-IV *Piloting*. The PCLs are quite direct:

What *Is?*

What *Isn't?*

This is, again, based on a high-level esoteric 'New Thought' exercise; but a Grade-V *Seeker* should not demonstrate any difficulty in running these simply worded PCLs in alternation to each other and increase their sense of overall *reality* on the present moment; differentiating, with light techniques, between that which *Is* and *Is-Not* in the present. When run effectively, this produces a state that literally would take hours and days of frustration off of whatever it is that folks use more "**Eastern**-style" forms of meditation to achieve. By cutting through a lot of the miscellaneous circuitry directly, a *Seeker* is able to apply a much greater level of *Actualized Awareness* to their higher-level goals on the *Pathway*.

---

‡   Alternatively, this could be run as: "Get the *idea...*"

As a conceptual-objective exercise to supplement: a *Seeker* can apply their attention to a small object or wall and run the following PCLs until their own satisfaction:

1. Get the concept that it is there.

2. Get the concept that it is not there.

3. Hold both concepts simultaneously.

This is all applied in Grade-V to free up 'Attention-Units' and take some focus off of the direct exploration of the *Backtrack*. An increase of *Actualized Awareness* is necessary to peel back more layers and determine where a *Seeker* is at—what starting point or entry-point onto the *Backtrack* is most appropriate or accessible. Usually, it involves some of the turbulence already encountered in *Beta-Defragmentation*, which is why it is a good idea to keep quality written records of that work, as well. Because as fragmented as it all might seem, there is some **epicenter** that it all surrounds; there is something that underlies the patterns and cycles that an individual finds themselves in —and it is the uncovering and handling of "what lies beneath" that we have targeted as the goal of our upper-level Systemology Wizard work. Because it is *that* which is hidden behind all of these other layers of fragmentation that we are ultimately after in order to achieve our true and destined *Ascension*.

Therefore, the computations and considerations, the *implanting* and *programming*, all of this is basically geared toward a particular direction for the *Seeker*. The *track* provides the sense of time-space illusion that is necessary to provide a sense of continuance and various **phases** on different cycles. So, behind the expressions inherent in Human behavior in *this* society, there is an underlying "goals and roles" program playing out for the *Seeker*. In spite of the entrapment within a prison reality, the *Alpha-Spirit* is still playing a *game*—however much **enforced** that participation may be at this present time.

Participation in a *game*—be it the experience of *this* existence, or some other *game* involving choices—is all about an interaction between the individual and a set of possible '*conditions*'. It is the manner in which these aspects are confronted and handled that differentiates the experience of one **player** from another. More of this **Game Theory** will be handled in Grade-VI, but it is just as relevant here and now, especially when we have decided to blow the cover off of the *Backtrack*. At any rate, the handling of the conditions in '*Life*' is a strong indicator as to *what* an individual is actually attempting to accomplish or is *implanted* to strain for or be plagued by as a preoccupation.

This sequence of "preoccupations" and "goals" is something that *Backtrack* processing is intended to reveal and it is quite relevant for an individual to be retracing the unique steps of their spiritual descent. We have uncovered various patterns, but all individuals have not walked the same *track* simultaneously to each other—and for that reason, at present, each *Seeker* is likely at a different phase of a different cycle than the next. Although we have found that there are definitely some strong similarities between those *Seekers* that feel the "calling" more directly toward this work at this particular point in Human history. Some of us have been at *this* together, before—and some of us have had our *tracks* intertwine more often than others. But we are all still carrying our own unique 'Spiritual Timeline' that brings us here now.

So, the PCLs for this may be run *Solo*, but generally work best with a communication flow. And our intention is to bring that which the individual is "*stuck*" in—or *on*—into view without inciting excessive turbulence. They are:

SPOT a persistent condition.

\ WHAT have you done about that?

It may also to run considerations for this PCL regarding one's own observational data: the cross-flow circuit about others. This is also helpful for shifting the flow of attention for a while after using the first PCL for *Self* repetitively in a systematic processing session. It would basically run as:

SPOT a condition that has persisted for another.

\ WHAT have they done about that?

Often times the program of "roles and goals" that we carry with us has many inherent attitude and/or behavior traits associated with it. There may be indications of this found in our opinionated determinations or considerations about others—or about a certain type of person as a "terminal"—that may not only stem from specific incidents taking place with others on the *Backtrack,* but also the artificial incident-like data that is incorporated into whatever program we are running: be it the *holy avenger* or the *stoic monk* or whatever archetypal **game** we are playing at. So, in addition to the previous PCLs, some other insights might arrive from running:

SPOT a deeply held belief.

\ WHAT have you done about that?

So, therefore as a general rule for Grade-V: if a *Seeker* has difficulties with these Route-4V prerequisites, they should return their attention to Grade-III and Grade-IV[‡] work; and if there are no difficulties in running these PCLs, and more preferably, the individual has an increased sense of their 'Spiritual Power' as a *Presence* and *Awareness* and an increased reality on the existence of the *Backtrack*, then they may officially continue their work with Route-4C and the remainder of Grade-V.

---

‡ Our experience with systematic processing shows that particular attention should be paid to unfinished work in the areas of *responsibility, ethics* and especially *justification* from Grade-IV—"Route-3E", "Route-3Y" &tc.

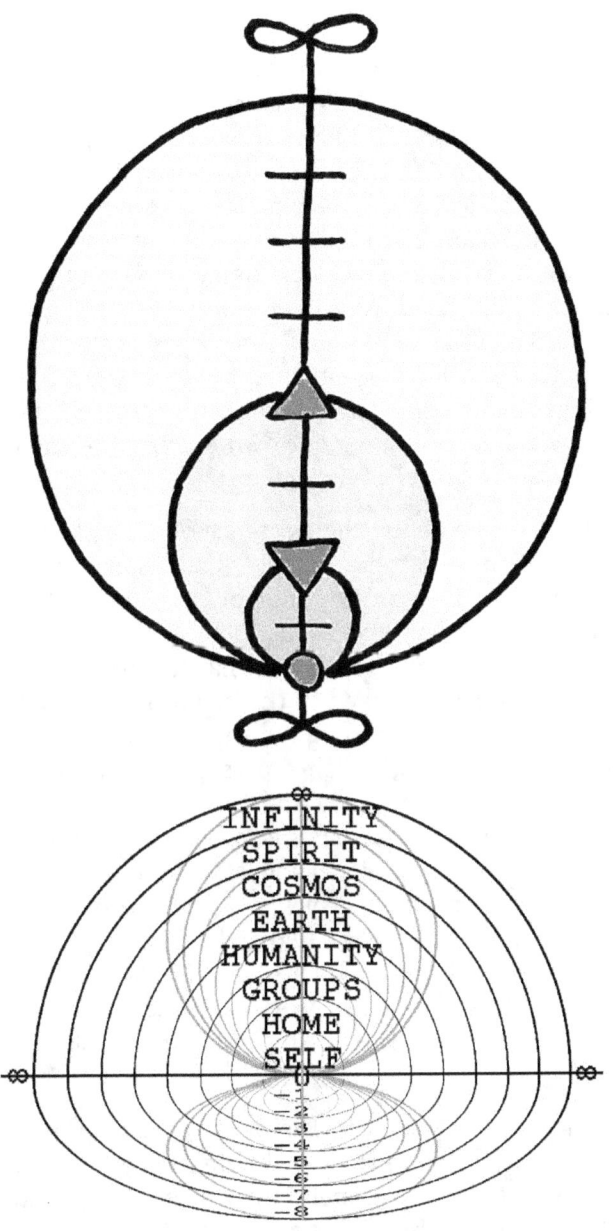

∞
INFINITY
SPIRIT
COSMOS
EARTH
HUMANITY
GROUPS
HOME
SELF
0
−1
−2
−3
−4
−5
−6
−7
−8

△ △ △ △ △ △

The subject of *implants* occurs twice directly in Grade-IV: in Unit-3 of *"Metahuman Destinations"* and also in *"Way of the Wizard"* (**Liber-3E**). The two works were prepared a year apart from one another and in was quite noticeable that our revision of the basic pattern had improved. The Unit-3 information from 2020 was updated in late 2021; both were *workable,* however our improvements simply made our additional experiments work *better.* But, we've only just mentioned the *implants* in passing before and never really treated them directly in systematic processing. This means that they are not necessarily understood widely even among our own *Seekers* entering upon the Grade-V segment of the *Pathway.*

In Grade-IV, we define the existence of an *implant* as the "platform" and "pattern" on which additional *imprinting* is based. This is accurate, but not necessarily the only data we can understand about them at this juncture of work. In *Liber-3E,* we established that the most basic patterns were directly linked to the eight **'Spheres of Existence'** that we treat in our philosophy and variations of our Standard Model, which represent the harmonics of *Beta-Existence.* Of course, we also found out that these harmonics repeat themselves at a higher-level; basically with Sphere-One in *Beta* being a lower-frequency harmonic of Sphere-Nine ("Ethics") in *Alpha.* This was found to be the case with Sphere-Two and a theoretical Sphere-Ten ("Aesthetics") as well. This material from *"Way of the Wizard"* (*Liber-3E*) is quite worthwhile to review before applying systematic processing to defragment *implants* directly.

Implants show up on the *Backtrack,* particularly in the "between-lives" areas that are intentionally hidden from common-view. We have maintained a very long existence and carry the accumulated evidence for this as our *'Spiri-*

tual Timeline', and during this long time-span, we have been in various positions, at one time or other, to control one another. Most commonly, we have found efforts on the *Backtrack* to *implant* people in order to "enslave" them, or *implant* them with "ethics" to stop them from doing various things. Efforts to control these aspects of social life—to make people loyal or enslave them—continues even in our present society, today. Of course, our methods today are quite *light* in comparison to the type of high-power technology and electronic-waves that must have been involved with establishing the original *implant platforms* aeons ago on the *Backtrack*.

In this *Beta-Existence, implanting* is commonly accomplished by hitting the *Alpha-Spirit* with electronic-waves in combination with operative **"command lines"** that are *implanted.* They are *implanted* "postulates" that do not actually originate with the *Alpha-Spirit* themselves. Most of the ones discovered and listed in Grade-IV are quite specific to our experience as a "POV" fixed on surviving as *organic-life* in this local Universe, on this local planet. These *implants* are rooted more strongly in the make-up of what we consider to be an "identity" in this *Beta-Existence. Implants* are certainly more influential for the "long haul" across the *Backtrack* than an incidental *imprint*; and as I've explained before, much of the "suffering" and "turbulence" associated with the average *imprint* is due to an entire "stack" of related *imprints* all "chained" together with some type of *implant* as a base or foundation platform. It's kind of like how the effects from the rules of a *game* only seem devastating relative to the **investment** an individual has in that *game*; since outside of and exterior to the *game*, such and such would be deemed irrelevant. These *implants* are a part of what is actually keeping us *in* the *game*-mode in the first place.

Implanting-Incidents are quite different from *Imprinting-Incidents.* For one: *implanting* generally takes place "between-lives" whereas the *imprinting* occurs during the course of an incarnation. *Implanting* is an artificial install-ation of *imprinting* that gives the sense of having an ex-perience that one did not actually have, or the formation of a postulate or consideration that the individual did not actually originate. *Imprints* usually contain imagery and *facets* from an event or incident that has taken place, whereas *implants* are generally filled with complex pat-terns, false images and various other misinformation em-bedded to keep the nature and existence of the *Implant* (and the related incident) hidden from discovery by the *implanted* individual themselves.

If what I'm describing seems drastic or extreme—well, it *is*, but you have to take into account just how much en-ergy it would take to fix something to an *etheric being* that would persist in existence with the *Alpha-Spirit* con-tributing to its creation along the way, thinking that it is its own. The actual effects of the *Implants* can be reduced to the level of a bothersome television commercial if an individual is maintaining high enough *Actualized Aware-ness.* We might go as far as to say that the level of control and influence that they possess over an individual is in proportion to the level of *Actualized Awareness* that the in-dividual maintains. You can see, then, why we push for that development alongside the technical training.

Most of the turbulence associated with exploring the Sys-temology of *Implants* erupts from things that an individu-al has done that are also hidden from readily available view. We've all been on both sides of this on the *Back-track*; we've all been on the 'giving' and 'receiving' ends of this, and there is a considerable amount of turbulence associated with the 'giving' end, as well. At one time or another, we have all been participants in a society that believed that this type of *Implanting* was critical to the ideal survival and continuance of the society, or that planet, or that galaxy, or even that Universe.

Most of the stuff that has run wild and rampant as things developed along the *Backtrack* did not start off with malicious intents; but as we know from just looking around the present society, just about anything can be used to do something else—for example, just about anything can be weaponized. Just within the last one-hundred years, our own Intelligence Community in the United States has made vast experimental use of various forms of electronic-implanting using commands combined with **symbols**, various triggers, and the use of altered states and such. Just this past year, I released the volume titled "*The Metaphysics of Stranger Things*" (*Liber-011*) through the Systemology Society, which discusses some of that. The point is, we should not be so surprised to have found these types of things taking place on the *Backtrack* at a wide-scale, when we conduct the same type of work here on Earth in present society. Most of your typical *dystopian fantasy* and *science-fiction* reflects very light versions of the type of themes, conditions and situations that have even taken place on the *Backtrack* "a long time ago in a galaxy far away."

Regarding Grade-V, *Implants* interfere with quality "past-life recall"—and it is true that things that are *implanted* do maintain a residual effect so long as the contents are not confronted *As-It-Is*. There are certain "items" used to associate the *implanted* material—and if these "terminals" appear as *facets* of other *imprints,* they will not fully "reduce" unless the actual content of the *Implant* is *spotted*. The content of typical *Beta-Existence* implants generally follow a pattern; so that is of benefit to us, because Grade-V does not include the type of training that would be necessary for a *Seeker* to determine much of this from scratch.

The most basic or direct approach for Route-4C, regarding the *processing-out* of an *Implant* platform, is to "*spot*" or "*imagine*" each "command item" (and "object-item") in the 'programming sequence' until it ceases to have any influential effect on the *Seeker*. Some of you will be happy to know that this type of upper-level work often runs best *Solo*, since most of you now have been working along the *Pathway* that way; and for those that *Pilot* others, this type of *Solo-Flying* can be demonstrated to a *Seeker* so they can *run* it on their own.

Ultimately, a *Co-Pilot* is there to *assist* a *Seeker* until they are of such a level that they can *Fly-Solo*; and Grade-V is that threshold—although in professional practice, the *Seeker* still operates under the supervision of an experienced *Pilot*. This is another reason for getting in the practice of taking good notes on whatever transpires during a systematic processing session. When applied professionally with a GSR-Meter (as in Route-4G), the material is still *Co-Piloted*, but eventually a *Seeker* is able to learn how to operate the session and monitor *GSR-biofeedback* simultaneously while alone.

Defragmenting—or 'processing-out'—the content of an *Implant* is to alternate attentions with "spotting the item" and "spotting something in the room." A *Pilot* can direct these as PCLs, but when *Flying-Solo*, it is simply a consistent and repetitive shifting of attentions between "spotting the item" and "spotting something in the room." The *command-item* is sometimes associated with a physical "object-item"—but is essentially a "**command**." And these commands were not *implanted* in English, but we are simply treating them as most appropriate for our practical purposes even when the literal statements seem strange. So, when you "*spot*" an "item," it's important to get a strong sense of the *implanted intention* 'underlying' the "Item."

This is essentially how one would reverse the effects of *implanted* commands found in today's "brainwashing"— because we are essentially reversing the process; a reverse-hypnosis, so to speak. When an individual is *impla-*

nted, they are generally under duress or another altered state that promotes low-*Awareness* and then the command-sequence is given along with the attention fixed on a particular item, or fixed on something, at any rate. In this case, we perform the same procedure and systematically "unfix" the attention from the command and any other items associated. There is a lot more technical data on this that I want to get into before we are done for the day, so we will continue this segment on Route-4C in the next lecture.

.: LECTURE SEVEN :.
IMPLANTS ON THE BACKTRACK—PART 2
("ROUTE-4C")
19, MARCH 2023

While we have been aware of the existence of metapsy-chological and metaspiritual *Implants* at the Systemology Society since the very beginning, these Grade-V lectures are the first time we are handling the subject directly—and in conjunction with the *Backtrack*. This is primarily because a *Seeker* can only have an appreciation of what *Implanting* is if they have a reality on the fact that the *Backtrack* exists. Without the idea of "past-lives" and "between-lives" periods, the existence of such *Implanting* would seem like an anomaly, when in fact, the opposite is true, and *every single* individual inhabiting the planet today has been subjected to it on their own 'Spiritual Timeline'.

'New Thought' practitioners and those in the field of "transpersonal" or "motivational" psychology have known for a century or more that the "goals" and "purposes" maintained by an individual will significantly affect their thought-patterns and behaviors in life. Most of the time, the therapeutic efforts have all been aimed at simply making the individual more comfortable in their circumstances, whereas we are now more concerned with systematically looking at the underlying reasons for these inclinations and assumption of various "roles"—particularly when they seem to affect the actual 'Free Will' and true 'Self-determinism' of the individual.

The standard-issue Human Condition also shares some *Implanting* patterns with other 'earthbound' life forms, particularly the animal kingdom. For example, one need only spend a little time with dogs to realize they carry the "*To Eat* is *To Know*" command-item. And they tend to operate in a similar sequence down the line of a platform, such as *"To Eat is To Be Alive"* and so on. And then usually this is tied to some iconic archetype or *Beingness* form—such as *"To Be a Tiger"* or something, just as an example. Or, maybe, for the goal *"To Keep Things Clean,"* you might have the role of *"A Housekeeper"* as a "terminal"—and thus *"To Be A Housekeeper"* would be one phase of this cycle on a goals sequence-chain.

Prior to this—for example, in another lifetime—they might have been a *"High Society Lady,"* but with the decline of that goal, they enter a new phase as the *"Housekeeper"* for example—because maybe they decided *that* was thing to be now, after countless lives of their husband running around with the housekeeper, or something like that. But then, eventually that "role" degrades as well, and perhaps eventually the individual is willing to be nothing more than a *"bag-lady"* or something like that; that becomes the extent of their willingness and reach. You see how this can go? Then, if the cycle is not recognized, it may just be repeated again; the *"pauper"* desires to be a *high-society fellow*, then meets with betrayal, and begins dwindling down the chain again. These are the kinds of cycles that get played out on the *Backtrack*.

The *Implanted* "goals and roles" of the *Backtrack* that seem to motivate our inclinations and thought-patterns *never actually* yield the satisfactory results that we are after while assuming each of these *"Identity-Phases."* They are always taken up on a chained-sequence in opposition to something else and later we are in opposition to the very goal itself until we shift to another cycle. But the pattern seems to suggest that the direction is always downward—that the spiral is also dwindling. This is what creates the turbulent energy and dark heavy masses that have jumbled up our *Awareness* of the *Backtrack*.

Now, ideally, if you were applying Route-4C to systematic processing with a *GSR-Meter* (for Route-4G), you could simply go down a prepared list for *"spotting"* each of these "items" and checking to see if there is any "charge" registered on the **biofeedback** *device.* You would then alternate *"spotting"* the "item" and *"spotting"* something in the room until the "item" is no longer registering. It may be more time-consuming and challenging to practice this with *'intuition'* alone—getting a *'sense'* for how various "items" make you feel—but it can be done.

Route-4C for *Implants* is, in many ways, similar to the handling of incidents, but some efficiency with former Grade-IV procedures and Wizard Level-0 techniques becomes key in this instance. The ideal goal for this procedure would be to reach with *Awareness* and contact the time on the *Backtrack* when the "item" was actually *implanted* and *"spot"* it there. Until there is an increased certainty on this ability, a *Seeker* can still get effective results with "conceptual running"—such as "get the concept of" or "get a sense of" or "get the idea of." A *Class-4 Pilot* should be familiar with this from previous training.

Biofeedback responses take place whether an individual is "metering" it or not. It does take some practice to get a 'sense' for when you've hit on something, or when something is reduced. At this juncture, without treating Route-4C with a *GSR-Meter*, a *Seeker* should do the best they can. It may require a bit of "mental" hunting around to really make good contact with an *Implant-Item.* When *Awareness* has connected with that particular channel, the *Seeker* may sense the energetic-mass or there may be the sensation of pressure somewhere—the sense that there is a resistance or something pushing against, either as an energy or some feeling of **protest**.

Remember that these *Implants* are enshrouded in enough confusion and mystery to keep an individual from discovering them. However, getting some sensation or feeling may assist in confirming that contact is made. But sometimes it is not as obvious when an "item" is not in restimulation; so again, a *GSR-Meter*—as described in *"Way of the*

Wizard" (*Liber-3E*), and to a lesser extent in "*Systemology-180*"—can be of invaluable assistance. In either case, the *Seeker* continues "*spotting*" the "item" until the sensations of "pressure" or "uneasiness" have dissipated. Not only should there be, to some extent, a sense of "release of weight" as a processing end-point, but there should also be no inclination or urge to actually "obey" the *Implant* command-item on any level.

Similar to when *processing-out* other *imprinting-incidents* at Grade-V, if during a session the *Seeker* finds that after "*spotting*" the "item" a number of times that it seems to be getting "heavier" or "denser" or more solid or *charged* up, then try to reach back to an *earlier* time that the "command-item" was *implanted*. The truth is that the same *Implants* were used again and again; so, just like as when tracing back an *imprint*-chain, a *Seeker* must contact the *first* time that each "command-item" of an *Implant* was used on them, in order to get an erasure on the entire platform-pattern. By the way: when you sit back later and look at your notes on this conference—or examine these lecture transcripts—you will see that this procedure is not nearly as complicated as it is to properly communicate the instructions this way up here in front of you. It is definitely deserving of additional study and review and practice by you later.

Now, there is also the possibility that in following along this procedure you run into a situation where an *Implant-Item* is feeling "heavier" and yet there doesn't seem to be an earlier *Implanting-Incident*. In this case, the most common reason is that some fragmented or turbulent "charge" has been left on a previous "item" from the same platform-pattern. This is what we mean when fragmentation is contacted in a systematic processing session and then "passed-by" or "by-passed" without being confronted *As-It-Is* before a *Seeker* moves on. So, if this happens, and it is common even in expertly *Piloted* sessions—

particularly without a *GSR-Meter*—then it is critical to trace your processing steps back a few "items" and check to see if there is some residual energetic-mass still on the *line.* If so, then just *process-out* the "item" further.

When handling *Implants,* a predefined platform-pattern list is *processed-out*—as I've just described—until there is no longer any energetic-mass (charge, turbulence, &tc.) present on it. A *Seeker* should not be feeling any fatigue or "heaviness" or hypnotic-like states at the end-point of *Implant* processing. This should also allow a *Seeker* to be able to casually look over the entire listed contents of an *Implant* without any reactions, significances or importances attached to any of the *Implant-Items.*

Δ Δ Δ Δ Δ Δ Δ

Heavier *Implants* are so well disguised or shielded that they cause an individual to "flinch" away—or *withdraw*—from an encoded unpleasantness that is embedded within the *Implant.* Any time that an individual is in a position to discover the truth about what's going on "behind the curtain" it seems that they reactively retract from it. For example, during some of our earlier Wizard Grade experiments—going back even to 2019, we worked with our more advanced Systemologists that could provide a heightened "presence" to research sessions—we used the PCL of "what would happen if you *knew*" and "what would happen if you *found out*"; just very generally stated like that, you know? And would you believe, the sense of dread and sometimes fear that emerged from this—it was quite obvious that a person was programmed to think they would "die" if they really *knew.*

It should be obvious, then, that *Implanting* would likely include commands to "kill yourself" embedded within them, if the individual was to "find out" about it. Now, of course, that does not mean that is what the reactive behavior would *actually* be. These *Implanted* "suggestions" become a nuisance to an ideal high quality of experiencing existence, but the "command-items" are not generally obeyed blindly. In fact, something of this nature would only seem absolutely solid in present-time to an individual that was experiencing an extreme level of low-*Awareness* "psychosis"—and perhaps this has something to do with it, though I've given up on trying to revise the understanding of existing schools on mental health.

At any rate, the effects of *Implanting* seem to wear off with our increased attention on its existence until we experience an "erasure" of it altogether. Even when they are newly *Implanted*, the extreme nature of the "command-items" are designed simply so they will "*stick.*" We are, again, talking about an *eternal spirit*—and it takes violently *Implanting* the *Alpha-Spirit* with "*To Know* is *To Die*" heavily, many times over just to get any continuance of effect in perpetuity thereafter on the *Track*. It takes that much extreme overkill just to get someone to a point where the individual feels "uneasiness" whenever the content or discovery of the *Implant* is approached. So, don't let the fragmentation fool you: this work is simply encoded to give the feeling that it would be dangerous to remember.

It should be understood that the *Implants* themselves have never been exceptionally powerful in the traditional sense. It isn't so much a concern about the *Implants* and *Imprints* themselves that causes the issues, but rather the handling of them and the turbulent energy and heavy masses that ensue. For example, as in the case with marketing and advertising, we have only suggestions and propaganda. These in themselves are not where the "power" lies. They do, however, **incite** an individual to make certain postulates and considerations—and these of course are represented in the decisions we make about life. For example, a "command-item" about suicide and death if the *Implant* is discovered, is simply meant to get the individual to decide for themselves to forget about the *Implant* as an act of *'Self-protection'*. You see how that works? And there is a lot of this type of stuff on the *Back-track*.

Since Route-4C is generally processed *Solo*, the previous recommendation still stands concerning the use of a card or piece of paper to cover any prepared lists of "items"— just as you would if "Self-Processing" the PCLs out of one of our books. When using prepared lists, the "items" are *"spotted"* as if they are PCLs until they are defragmented. Moving a sheet of paper down one "item" at a time not only makes it easier to keep your place on a list, but more importantly, to keep attention on only *one* "item" at a time. And you still alternate your attention with something in the room—but you're not racing back and forth, but you also don't need to "linger" on one or the other. You want to *"spot"* something and notice something about it, thereby actually applying your *Awareness*; and then take your attention off of it and *"spot"* something in the room, noticing some detail about it. Let's face it, you're playing "mental" "peek-a-boo" with the *Implant* all stealth-like; picking away at it with each application of attention without remaining in its hypnotic-gaze long enough to get fully restimulated. And then it's gone.

Even if you have not completed an entire platform-pattern in a single processing session, if you find yourself feeling particularly "good" during the work, it's a good time to end-session and take a break. There are several reasons to do this. Of course, we like to end-session on a positive note; when things are seeming brighter and we are feeling "good" and thinking clearer. It is possible that the remaining platform-pattern has defragmented—of which case there would be no "charge" on the remaining "items" if they were checked; but sometimes this is also inherent in getting a big processing "win" from one of the "items"—and the sense of "relief" that is experienced from reaching that point can overshadow the fragmentation that still remains on the platform. So, a *Seeker* thinks the whole platform has "erased" because of their sense of "elation" when it may not be. So, for this reason we say: take a break.

After you *process-out* all the *Implant-Items* of a platform-pattern, complete the procedure by "*spotting*" any postulates or considerations that you made at the time of the *Implanting-Incident.* To carry this even further for more proper A.T. application, see if you can "*spot*" any times that you *Implanted* another being with that pattern —or at the very least had wanted people *Implanted* with it. This will help eliminate any residual from the "erasure" and provides a proper end-point for the procedure.

We're going to use the "Suicide Pattern" as a demonstration *Implant-Platform* because it is related to what we've been talking about and also is quite a basic pattern as these things go—not even really a complete "platform" in itself, because we find that it is often attached to the beginning and/or ending of other prominent platform-patterns that are common to the standard-issue Human Condition. Not all "command-items" are this extreme. Again, the reason this pattern is added to other completely unrelated platforms is because of the tendency for an individual to want to forget about it. So, it is a good one to practice with by itself. When more of this type of work is conducted at the Systemology Society and collected and **codified**, I'm sure we'll label and designate the various patterns and platforms, but for now, this is simply known as the "Suicide Pattern." Each of these lines is considered a "*command-item.*"

Δ Δ Δ Δ Δ Δ Δ

[The following two pages should not be casually read.]

1. To Know About This Is To Disbelieve It.[*]

2. To Know About This Is To Forget About It.

3. To Know About This Is To Become Insane.

4. To Know About This Is To Become Unconscious.

5. To Know About This Is To Be Unaware.

6. To Know About This Is To Be Sick.

7. To Know About This Is To Die.

8. To Know About This Is To Kill Myself.

9. To Talk About This Is To Disbelieve It.

10. To Talk About This Is To Forget About It.

11. To Talk About This Is To Become Insane.

12. To Talk About This Is To Become Unconscious.

13. To Talk About This Is To Be Unaware.

14. To Talk About This Is To Be Sick.

15. To Talk About This Is To Die.

16. To Talk About This Is To Kill Myself.

17. To Find Out About This Is To Disbelieve It.

18. To Find Out About This Is To Forget About It.

19. To Find Out About This Is To Become Insane.

20. To Find Out About This Is To Become Unconscious.

21. To Find Out About This Is To Be Unaware.

22. To Find Out About This Is To Be Sick.

23. To Find Out About This Is To Die.

24. To Find Out About This Is To Kill Myself.

25. To Remember This Is To Disbelieve It.

---

[*] This list is reproduced here from the handout given at the conference. Only a few examples were read from the list at the lecture. It is not advisable to casually read the list unless it has been systematically processed or is *being* actively systematically processed-out.

26. To Remember This Is To Forget About It.

27. To Remember This Is To Become Insane.

28. To Remember This Is To Become Unconscious.

29. To Remember This Is To Be Unaware.

30. To Remember This Is To Be Sick.

31. To Remember This Is To Die.

32. To Remember This Is To Kill Myself.

33. To Think About This Is To Disbelieve It.

34. To Think About This Is To Forget About It.

35. To Think About This Is To Become Insane.

36. To Think About This Is To Become Unconscious.

37. To Think About This Is To Be Unaware.

38. To Think About This Is To Be Sick.

39. To Think About This Is To Die.

40. To Think About This Is To Kill Myself.

Δ Δ Δ Δ Δ Δ

Much like we can assume that life existed on Earth predating the Human records written by Human hands at the inception of this present version of 'earthbound' civilization, the *Backtrack* only exists for as long as it has been maintained as a recording. Relatively speaking, this is approximately 4.3 quadrillion years long—at least this is what answers up in Route-4G and other upper-level experiments. Whether or not the presently accessible portion of the *Backtrack* is *actually* 4.3 quadrillion years long, or simply contains a record that makes it appear as such, this at least gives you some idea of what we are dealing with. Of course, the *Alpha-Spirit* has been around for much longer than that, but it did not always carry a Mind-System in tow. We *have* what we *have* to work with at this juncture, and it primarily begins—as an accessible record—when the *Alpha-Spirit* started getting *Implanted* and recording *Imprints.*

Another phenomenon we discovered early on in our systemological research, is the idea of descending and condensing Universes—something explored conceptually in Grade-IV, particularly in **Liber-3C** (Unit-3) of "*Metahuman Destinations*" and, of course, "*Imaginomicon*" (*Liber-3D*). We have always been concerned with what is "workable" in our Systemology—what works to provide the results we are after—rather than adhering to anything that comes up as Absolute Fact. Of course, since the beginning, our systematic methods, applied philosophy and Standard Models have all provided enough room to calculate various theories ahead of time, and often with predictable results. What I mean is that our research and development has consistently been ahead of itself, consistently producing *realizations* at one tier that are only effectively workable once we reach a higher level to operate on. This has certainly been the case with the *Backtrack*, which also provided the greater certainty that had been missing on the handling of *Implants* and a greater understanding of

Universes that the *Alpha-Spirit* experienced previous to the present version of *Beta-Existence*.

We have long suspected that since the *Hebrew Kabbalah*—that is so popular in mysticism—was, in fact, based on the much older Mesopotamian lore of the *"Ladder of Lights"* and *Star-Gates,* that there must be some relationship between the sequential ordering of the Universes that represent the descent of the *Alpha-Spirit* to its current state. Given all these additional years of examining the *'Arcane Tablets'* and their relationship to the various classifications of levels and Gates and layers of fragmentation, we were able to arrive at a much more concise "map" for the descent of the *Alpha-Spirit* through various Universes. It even demonstrates the shortening cycles that seem apparent to each subsequent Universe.

Although this information is still subject to change pending additional ongoing upper-level work, I feel confident in at least presenting this part of our Wizard-Grade "Secret Doctrine of the Cosmos" as a handout for this conference and, of course, the published lecture transcripts at a later time. So, this is the most basic progression of Universes as it relates to both the Gates and the Kabbalah, as it is generally understood today.

8. <u>Infinity</u>

7. <u>Home Universe</u>

6. <u>800 Quadrillion Years Ago – estimated</u>
   "Games Universe" (Jupiter/Chesed)

5. <u>400 Quadrillion Years Ago – estimated</u>
   "Motions Universe" (Mars/Geburah)

4. <u>64 Quadrillion Years Ago - estimated</u>
   "Symbols Universe" (Sun/Tiphareth)

3. <u>4.3 Quadrillion Years Ago</u>
   "Implant-Penalties Universe" (Venus/Netzach)

2. <u>2.8 Quadrillion Years Ago</u>
    "Thought-Energy Universe" (Mercury/Hod)

1. <u>200 Trillion Years Ago</u>
    "Magic Kingdom Universe" (Moon/Yesod)

0. <u>86 Trillion Year Ago</u>
    "Beta-Existence/Physical Universe" (Malkuth)

This model corresponds perfectly with the understand-ing that we have of the *Gates* and the *Kabbalah* from *this* side of *this* version of *"Beta-Existence."* This means that the lore applies to **correspondences** that are really only relevant to those 'earthbound' and/or fixed to *this* Phys-ical Universe. It is, of course, an ancient "map" out from here, oriented from this viewpoint. If it were to have been presented, for example, in a previous Universe, it would have been modeled after a completely different ce-lestial or planetary paradigm; aligned to a completely dif-ferent type or form of *Kabbalah.* Because prior to the es-tablishment of *this* Physical Universe, the *continuity zero-point* or lowest-common manifest expression would have been the foundations of the *"Magic Universe."*

Now, with the additional condensation of this *Beta-Exist-ence,* the *"Magic Kingdom Universe"* is an **inter-dimen-sional** "fairyland" by comparison—and this is by no coin-cidence, since it actually *is* the archetype for that prover-bial "Otherworldly Space" that was once so well under-stood and experienced by us in the distant past. I men-tion all of this here, because a serious *Seeker* intent on ex-ploring the depths of the *Backtrack* is likely to start run-ning into remnants from these other Universes, if not re-collections directly. Another reason I mention this stuff is to offer some guidelines on what to find some certainty on for yourself. Because too often a *Seeker* can get appre-hensive about higher-level work regarding operating in-dependent of a body or leaving this Universe or *Ascension,* and they start to wonder if there is anywhere else to go—

and anything else to *Be*—beyond what they've been *Implanted* to perceive.

For thousands of years, members of the Human civilization have sought a means to reclaim what was forgotten; to access the ultimate Gateway through which we first entered this Universe; to turn around and return to the Source. The heavy weights that bind our Spiritual Power and our true knowledge of ourselves has become too great to carry along with us any further; and fearing a descent—realizing the pattern that we are headed toward in descending to yet another lower plane after this one— the ancients have left us with obscure 'clues' and archaic 'maps', hoping to give us enough sense to remind ourselves of what we have chosen to forget. Perhaps for the first time in our current Human history, we have finally rediscovered the Hidden Key that will provide us with The Way Out—and when the opportunity for that ultimate *Ascension* finally presents itself, perhaps for the first time in our present cycle on the 'Spiritual Timeline', we will have the good sense to take it.

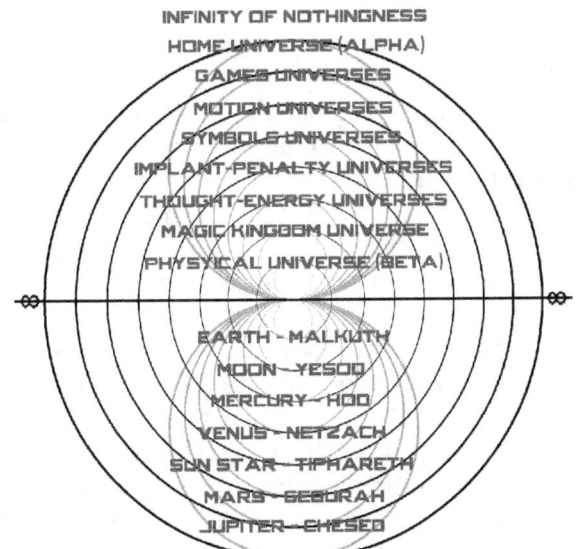

.: LECTURE EIGHT :.
GOALS IMPLANTED ON THE BACKTRACK
FINAL LECTURE
("ROUTE-4Y")
19, MARCH 2023

Alright—so, we've come up to the final lecture for this conference on the *Backtrack*; given too, a few of you have to duck out this afternoon to travel back to your *default* worlds. Rather than give just a summary of the weekend, I figure we will take advantage of this time together and plug forward into a discussion of some of the more experimental work we are doing for Grade-V. Most of what I've shared at this conference will require more research time this year before developing an appropriate "self-guiding" workbook. However, I've already spent the last year collecting all this in a vacuum; you know, up in the Ivory Tower of the Mardukite Academy—and in order to get any further **feedback** beyond that, we needed to at least get this foundation set, and firmly establish just what point we are at on the *Pathway*.

To clarify from earlier: the previous Grades—and materials collected in "*Systemology-180*"—are used first and foremost in cleaning up the handling of *this* life before the *Backtrack* is officially introduced to a *Seeker*. It's called "Beta-Defragmentation" for a reason. Of course, from a *Piloting* perspective, we find *expert* handling of "Beta-Defragmentation" results from Grade-V—because now an individual begins to understand the "*Why?*" for a lot of the fragmentation experienced in *this* lifetime. The *Backtrack* is important, then, for *Class-4 Pilots* to understand— as well as *Seekers* "*Flying-Solo*" on their ascent. But for a *Seeker* that is only being processed—and not taking the training routes—you can "run" systematic processing for "Beta-Defragmentation" without actually addressing the reality of "past-lives" or the *Backtrack* directly. But if you expect to understand the anomalies of what you find in *this* life, *that* can only be understood by peeling back the layers of many lifetimes and inspecting what lies beneath.

If you recall—if you were here last year, or read *"Liber-3E"*—the final lectures given to close Grade-IV and open the research and experiment phase of Grade-V pertained to considerations for *"justification."* We called it Route-3Y, since we wanted to know the *"Why?"* that the *Seeker* is carrying around to "justify" their thought-patterns and behaviors in life. We didn't impose routes for **Ethics-Processing** just to install some arbitrary **"morals and dogma"** into the Pathway. This is what some low-*Awareness Seekers* thought when reviewing the Grade-IV to Grade-V crossover material for *"Way of the Wizard"* (*Liber-3E*); yet that material represented the missing piece that our regimen required to deliver the desired results of *Beta-Defragmentation.*

A full understanding of *Beta-Defragmentation* is probably not possible without taking the *Backtrack* into account. There are so many aspects to *Beta-Defragmentation* that don't make sense when operated on the consideration that *this* is the only "lifetime" that a *Seeker* has experienced as an *Alpha-Spirit.* The work up until this point stirs up considerations and **evaluations** that seem illogical as the individual's "ultimate solutions" for handling present-time life—and they *are* illogical; but they make more sense when one considers the lines of code and programming that they have emerged from on the *Backtrack.*

Consider all the various series of *Beta-Processing* training routes and techniques and the emphasis we placed on targeting certain types of information in systematic processing. Much of what we found most effective from previous Grades is now collected in *"Systemology-180"*—and what we've been doing is systematically examining *what* a *Seeker* is *doing* in this lifetime: what they will or won't communicate with; what they are *protesting*; what they want *changed*; what is *acceptable* as it is; what *must be*; what *must not*; who or what they could *help* and how; what *they've done*; what *others have done*; the whole Grand Tour, right? This is no random assortment of procedures we've been working with all these years.

And over these many years—in the establishment of a *Beta-Defragmentation* regimen—we have been peeling back layers, stripping off varying degrees of "unconsciousness" or "subconscious activity" or "automated mechanisms" of the Mind-System. It should also be evident that our Routes have been revolving around—circling—certain key "points" and *facets* that only seem to be handled with the *Backtrack*, or by someone that understands the phenomenon of the *Backtrack*. Some of these "keys" necessary to an individual's own defragmentation—*Actualization* or *Ascension*—are buried fairly deep under additional layers of *Implanting* and *Imprinting* that have taken place on the *Backtrack*. So, as a *Seeker* increases their certainty on existence and willingness to confront, more and more is able to be brought up into view.

Most fragmentation, by its very nature, is taking place "out-of-view" of the *Alpha-Spirit*; a whole mess of automated-circuitry of the Mind-System, plus whatever the *genetic-vehicle* has got going on—this is what defragmentation is meant to sort out. No other mainstream methods out there seem to accomplish that. And, it isn't so much that the *Implants* on the *Backtrack* have a really strong commanding value—that's not where the issues really are. I mean, they may have been strongly embedded on our *track*, but that's nothing compared to an individual's own power of *consideration*—the evaluations that the individual, the *Self*, makes as a result of the *Implanting* and *Imprinting*, well, this is how fragmentation takes place.

Many of the *Implanted* "command-lines" and *Imprinted* "considerations" turn into "command postulates" and "automated-circuitry" in the Mind-System. This replaces or substitutes a total *Actualized* experience of existence and fully *Self-determined* use of *Alpha-Thought* by the *Alpha-Spirit*. And as an individual relies more and more on the *Imprinting* of the Mind-System as a substitute for their own *Beingness*, there is a noticeable diminishing quality to the *Alpha-Spirit's* actualized "Ability"—what we might consider "Spiritual Ability"—as it descends farther and farther along this particular *track*.

There is also a misunderstanding that I overheard from discussions between lectures today that I should clear up. So, beneath everything I've discussed, there is *still* an *Alpha-Spirit's* own intended "basic purpose"—or else, what they had set out to do in the first place as a "command postulate" of *Alpha-Thought*. It is only because the *Alpha-Spirit* first decided to *have* "Goals" that the "*Goal-Implanting*" can be laid in later at all, more recently on the *Backtrack*. We term "earlier" on the *Backtrack* as to what happened before "later" events. So, "later" is more recently embedded stuff; the "earlier" is further into the past. At any rate, the decision to *have* "Goals" inevitably led to fragmentation, because it involves the "*fixation*" of *Attention* in such a way that develops on "automatic" or "subconsciously." And, of course, if an *Alpha-Spirit* can decide *to be "fixated" on a "Goal*," then they can, in some way, be convinced to be "fixated" on anything that can be presented as a *Goal*.

So, if we are going to be technical: the first command postulate in this direction by an *Alpha-Spirit* would be "*to have a goal*"—and then on that line, other "*Goal-Implanting*" is embedded to essentially "cave-in on" the individual's *Actual Goal*. The additional "suggestions" often get superimposed over one's own postulates—and the being is made to believe that they originated from themselves. But in actuality, the *facet* usually used to artificially encode this is "confusion." Additional confusion ensues—and also deeper *encoding* or *Implanting*—as more "layers" and energetic-mass is accumulated along these channels. And this "stuff" that is accumulated runs synchronous with the condensing and descending experience of "Universes" and also the proverbial "weights" that hold down an *Eternal Spirit* to a mundane life.

The trick to effective systematic processing is to bring what is laying "hidden" and operating on "automatic" up to a point of the individual's *Analytical Awareness*—for example, the "*Master Control Center*" or "4.0" on the Standard Model. We don't necessarily have to give everything the same degree of *scrutiny* that this vocabulary suggests, but it is only by *inspecting* the coding and programming "*As-It-Is*" that we might have a chance to undo—or discharge—any of the "subconscious" command-value it may have on us. By *realizing* that it is present, it is no longer able to continuously be created and maintain long-forgotten operation beneath-the-surface.

A *Seeker* has to be at a pretty high-*Awareness*—a high level of *Actualization*—to confront the *Backtrack* and discharge *Implanting*. An individual that has not been through *Beta-Defragmentation* (and/or only really has a general 'New Age' background) is going to "run" the "command lines" of an *Implant* like they are some kind of twisted "affirmations" or something. That's not what we're trying to do here. But such individuals are not likely to apply the right kind of high-power *attention* necessary—they end up doing little more than restimulate them. So, it's important at Grade-V that we don't discount or rush a *Seeker* through *Beta-Defragmentation* preliminaries, or propagate an idea that upper-level work will somehow adequately replace that solid foundation we have already developed.

Δ Δ Δ Δ Δ Δ Δ

So, now let us return to where we left off last year with "Wizard Level-1" and the subject of *"Justification."* In the March 2022 lectures, I stated that underlying the other processing we were developing at the time, there is a specific *"Justification Computation"* (evaluation or consideration) that is actually tied to the very "Goal-Line" that an individual is playing at. Of course, that is about as far as we got with that—although the basic "charge" on this is handled in systematic processing as Route-3Y for *Beta-Defragmentation*. But, this is only really understood in connection to *Implanting* and *Imprinting* on the *Backtrack*; therefore our treatment of it here will be Route-4Y.

The subject of "Justification" was not an arbitrary transition point for the Grades last year. Its handling brought us colliding right into the subject of *Goals* and the *Backtrack*—and ultimately the basement floor of what we now consider "Alpha-Defragmentation" for the upper-level Systemology Wizard Grades. A significant part of this new upper-level focus is to determine what a *Seeker* is actually "dramatizing" in their life—and how this relates to a string of experiences and chains of *Imprinting* on the *Backtrack*. We have worked off of an **axiom** for many years that: an individual doesn't move past the point that is misunderstood; and this includes misunderstood choices and decisions or postulates we chose, for whatever reasons, to forget along the way.

The term "backtrack" was selected for this gradient of work, because in essence, a *Seeker* is redirecting their attention *consciously* onto those points where their attention-units have been *stuck* and are held *unconsciously*; or to be more systematically precise in our terms, they are points where attention-units are fixed in the past *compulsively* and *automatically*. These points are where our "ZU"—the *Spiritual Awareness* we have as an *Alpha-Spirit*—are essentially "parked" on the *Backtrack*. These points are certainly not all local to *this* planet, galaxy or even *this* Universe, because of course, the *Alpha-Spirit* has never been truly located in *space-time*, except by its considerations of its own *Beingness*. So, this is spread all over the various existences we have experienced and gives us the substance for the entangled mass and turbulent energy of what has become an increasingly burdensome *track* to carry along with us along our 'Spiritual Timeline' as an *Alpha-Spirit.*

Route-3Y processing of "Falsehood" and "Justification" only peels back the layers that allow for using a more direct PCL for that process—which shows up in Route-30.

How Might a(n) ___ Make Themselves Right?

\ How Might a(n) ___ Make Others Wrong?

This represents the primary PCL emphasis for Route-4Y on the "terminal" for a *Goal*—along with any related exercise that helps achieve this result; or any rewording of the PCL that can eventually redirect the *Seeker* to understanding their own "personality-phase" or place on a *Goals*-sequence within the *Game-series* of conditions in *this* Universe. Once the *Backtrack* is opened up in processing, the PCLs must also be specifically worded and directed to "this lifetime"—especially if you are using *GSR-biofeedback* (Route-4G), because a meter will register on all accessible lifetimes unless attention is properly directed. So, once a possible *Goal* or primary "*Justification Consideration*" has been identified, the correct PCL for its inspection is:

In *This Lifetime,* How Would ___ Make You Right?

\ In *This Lifetime,* How Would ___ Make Others Wrong?

We had only scratched the surface of this last year and in the appendix of *Liber-3E*, but it's quite evident that this becomes a more significant area to clear up for our approach to *Alpha-Defragmentation.* In *Piloting,* the first PCL is only given once—and then the *Seeker* gives as many answers as comes to mind, until they start to repeat themselves or they simply run out of them. If attention requires redirection, the PCL can be repeated. Answers are **acknowledged**, but the *Pilot* should remain mostly silent for *Backtrack* work—except where two-way communication is needed to either discharge turbulence or to keep a *Seeker* "in session." Then the second PCL is given and the *Seeker* responds until that is *processed-out*, or they really start to answer the first PCL; of which you want to *flatten* anything from that by using the first PCL again. This is the way "alternating PCLs" should really be *run*, particularly at the Wizard Levels.

When applying this or any other former technique to the *Backtrack*—to increase one's reality or sense of the *Backtrack*—a *Pilot* merely needs to add:

WHAT *could* you confront about that?

\ WHAT would you *rather not* confront about that?

Assuming the *Seeker* has achieved enough "*Self-Honesty*" from *Beta-Defragmentation*, and is actually willing to answer the second PCL here, their level of confront will still continue to increase. I mean, if the person is just like, "oh, there's nothing I'm not willing to confront" when that is obviously not the case, then the PCLs take longer to get an individual to a *realization* or appropriate endpoint. However, a *Seeker* that lists off what they are unwilling to confront is still identifying these aspects or facets by placing any attention on them at all—and therefore their willingness to confront them will improve. As more of the *Backtrack* is elevated to, again, that point of *Analytical Awareness*—or *Actual Knowingness*—then more of it becomes available to the individual to access. We have already seen how this works with *this* lifetime, so in Grade-V, we are simply applying our Systemology to a higher gradient of application.

There is a difference between "listing for a single answer" and listing off answers to *process-out* all considerations along a channel. With a PCL like the "confront" example, we are generally just *processing-out* answers until a *Seeker* reaches a *realization,* runs out of answers, or attains a point where the considerations are no longer fixed in place or in one *flow*-direction. However, much of the Wizard-Level *"listing"* comes from 'New Thought' techniques to "root out" a singular answer—including ones that a *Seeker* may not be immediately *Aware* of, hence the supplemental exercises and additional PCLs that generally accompany each Route. The correct answer is also the key *realization* and 'end-point' of a particular process. When applying these techniques to Route-4G, a *GSR-Meter* may be used to verify the listed items.

When we talk about 'rightness' and 'wrongness' and what we "use" to make ourselves right and others wrong, we are treading on the essence of what *Ethics Processing* as Route-3E is intended to defragment. The aspects regarding *"Justification"* are particularly critical because of the amount of energetic-mass that develops on those lines. The *"Justification Consideration"* gets reinforced and validated the more it is used to literally 'justify' an individual's own experiences. The **associative** and self-validating tendency of the Mind-System will also prompt *finding* things in one's environment or experience that support these *justifications*—and a *Seeker* is not likely to have just one of these *justifications*. There will be a main one and there will also be many others that surround it. But, this is not a "chain" or "sequence" and therefore each one will have to be processed. Handling the main one will not eliminate the influence of other independently made *postulates* and *considerations*.

Δ Δ Δ Δ Δ Δ

Implanted conditions from the *Games*-series of "command-items" provide the "setting" and environment; also the general objective inherent in a particular *"game-field."* This has been going on for a very long time—and the progressive condensation and solidification of Universes is indicative of the numerous layers of additional *Implants* that are taken on with each tiered descent. But this only describes the *Games* and *Universes*—which become the main subject of our Grade-VI work. It does not, of course, take into account the other primary factor that strongly affects the individual, and that *is* the individual—the *"set"* within the *setting.* The individual takes on their own role as a *"Player"* in all of this, too; so we have the matter of treating the *"Goals"* and *"Personality-Phases"* that are individual to the *"Player"*—at their current stage or cycle of "play"—and how these developed from former "stages" and "cycles" and *phases.* Such is definitely within the realm of Grade-V and our Wizard Level-1 handling of the *Backtrack.*

The *"Justification Consideration"* is of particular importance for defragmentation, because although it is influenced by the succession of "goals and roles" experienced on the *Backtrack*, the consideration is attached to the *Seeker's* own *"Actual Goal"* at this stage in the game; it was a consideration that the *Seeker* made themselves, and therefore must be *spotted* and uncreated to be free of its fragmentation. A *"Justification Computation"* also does not get handled or *processed-out* directly by other Routes. This is why it is treated as 'separate' from the processing of *Implants* directly, because although these considerations are only really understood in relation to *Implants.* The handling of *Implants* by themselves, does not automatically *process-out* the *considerations* a person has made as a result of *Implants.* Likewise, the exclusive processing of the *computations* alone does not eliminate the beneath-the-surface influence of *Implants.* And unless *Implants* and *Computations* are understood together, a *Pilot* will have little chance in properly directing a *Seeker*. If the *Seeker* is left in a state of confusion about the existence of one in place of the other, very little forward progress will ensue.

Unlike a *"Goal,"* a consideration or computation is not a *"doingness"* or decision for "action"; it is, by definition, a *consideration...* and a *justification.* Where the "command-items" of a *"Goal"* are oriented toward postulates "To Be..." or "To Have..." or "To Do..."; one does not find that present in the *"Justification Computation."* The consideration is retained as a means or mode of "survival" within the conditions of the *"Game"*—and, of course, its *"flavor"* should be a hint at the "role" and *"phase"* the *Seeker* is presently using as a substitute for *Self* in order to be a *Player* in this *Game Universe.* Just as an *Alpha-Spirit* superimposes cumulative parameters for a "Shared Universe" over its own; so too is it convinced to substitute other "goals and roles" as considerations for its own *Beingness.*

Although an *Alpha-Spirit*, being 'eternal', has an innate ability to "survive" on its own, the conditions of the *Games Universes* are intended to *Implant* an idea that they are "in competition" with others in order to Survive at a more material level of *Beingness.* The most basic *Implant* of *this* Universe is "To Survive" by "Being Superior"—and thus we play out an entire sequence of "roles" through various lifetimes in our effort to accomplish this. Of course, none of these "roles" *actually wins*; the "winning" would result in a "No-Game" condition, or the end of a game—and thus, only the *pursuit* of a perceived "gain" will keep the *Player* "in" the *Game.* Thus, as most mystic philosophers often express: the *Game* is not meant to be won; it is meant to occupy our interests and attention. So, the key for *"Alpha-Defragmentation"* is to both *realize* and *break free* from the *Implantation* sequences that keep our *Awareness* fixed exclusively and compulsively to *this Game.*

Each individual in *this Game* maintains some aspect or *'Personality-Phase'* that is reinforced during the course of one's lifetime—or many lifetimes—that is used or maintained as a means of proving their superiority over others. It is a basic characteristic of an individual's *'Personality-Phase'*—and one that the *Seeker* will have an affinity for; something by which they are making themselves better than, or superior to, others. It might be: "to be smart" or "to be strong"—and this, again, ties into *Goals*. The superiority dynamic supports a *Game* of 'Domination of Others'—and this is the very *Game* that the more enlightened and *Actualized* among us, now and in history, are quite intent on *Ascending* from; rising above to experience *better Games* in relatively *higher Universes*.

This 'Superiority' *Game* of "Domination of Others" is literally *Self-destructive* to the *Alpha-Spirit* based on the low-Awareness that it remains suspended in—and the dwindling diminishing spiral that the course of the Human Condition is invariably following. In *this Game*, our best characteristics that we achieve on our journey begin to deteriorate because of the *Harmful-Acts* they are tied to and the **Hold-Out** of our own Spiritual Ability that we are left with. We've examined some of this in *"Way of the Wizard"* (*Liber-3E*) during our transition from Grade-IV—but without considering the entirety of the *Backtrack*, not all *Seekers* were as convinced of the relevance or significance of these aspects. Sometimes it really does require an *exterior* view to see the wide-angle picture; and that's what we want a *Seeker* to achieve in Grade-V: a greater certainty as we progress on the upper-level tiers of the *Pathway*.

"Rightness" and "Wrongness" are matters of *Ethics*—but at an *Alpha*-level of thought and existence, *Ethics* is equivalent to the 'Sphere of Personal Survival' we find mirrored at "1.0" (or *'First Sphere'*) on our Systemology models of *Beta-Existence*. Therefore, our perception of

'Rightness' and 'Wrongness' are tied to our means of Survival at a *Beta*-level. On a computational level, 'Rightness' *equals* 'Survival'. The continuation of our Survival is, of course, tied to our being 'Right' in evaluating our circumstances and adapting to various conditions, and so forth. Right?—In order to be 'Surviving', an individual is having to be *more* 'Right' *than* 'Wrong', just by the nature of the *Game*. So, there is a compulsion to be 'Right'. And when we are not, we have our *'Justifications'*.

As an extension application or alternative to the standard use of PCLs for *processing-out* the "*Justification Considerations*" of Route-4Y, we will suggest a "listing exercise" for *Co-Piloted* and *Solo* sessions. "Listing exercises"— whether you're using *GSR-biofeedback* or not—should be done when a *Seeker* is feeling good and can apply high-level *Awareness* and *presence* to a session. In a "listing exercise" you write down your answers to a "listing question" (in place of a standard PCL). If you start to feel low-energy move in—feeling 'heavy' or 'tired'—during an exercise, then you've "over-listed" and have missed the basic answer, which is already written on your list. But, if you are getting an increased sense of turbulence, anxiousness or irritability as you list, then you're just not hitting the right answer.

Finding "The Answer" is the *realization* or end-point of a 'listing exercise', but if you haven't found it in a session and a certain amount of listing has still left the *Seeker* feeling "okay" about things, then it can be left off and resumed later. It is also possible that looking back over the list—after a brief "cool-down" period—will actually yield that "The Answer" is there already; but if none of them "feel" right, then you continue. At any point during a 'listing exercise', if the *Seeker* gets a *realization* that such-and-such is the right answer, then you stop listing. If there is a major indecision between two or more answers, then it is likely that "The Answer" hasn't been listed yet.

And that all comprises about the best advice I can offer regarding the use of intuition for "*Listing*" in the absence of a *biofeedback* meter. In some cases and on some processing questions, the list will not be very long, assuming the *Seeker* has a general idea of "The Answer" from the start.

Δ Δ Δ Δ Δ Δ

Since we're going to make this "Final Lecture" an "Extended Lecture" rather than cut off here, let's just get right down into the procedure. The first 'listing question' is:

In *This Lifetime,* What Makes You Superior To Others?

Once you have "The Answer" or 'listing item', then you *process-out* the considerations by standard PCL procedure:

How does ___ make you superior?

\ How could you use it to make yourself right?

\ How could you use it to make others wrong?

The manner in which we handle 'Rightness' and 'Wrongness' in this respect may point toward the type of '*Personality-Phase*' or '*Implant-Item*' we are presently operating with. But ahead of that, and corresponding with it, we want to know exactly *what* it is about others that prompts us to unleash those characteristics we spoke of, and work competitively against others to gain our superiority. So, we have another 'listing question':

In *This Lifetime,* What Is It About *Them* That Makes *Them* So Wrong?

This 'listing' may loop back on the '*Justification Computation*', but may not. But, a *Seeker* may be fairly certain about 'The Answer'. Of course, if the 'listing item' isn't basic enough to support the type of consideration we are after, an additional 'listing question' may be applied that brings us back to one of our original PCL targets:

In *This Lifetime,* What Do You Use To Make Others Wrong?

The overall consideration that is arrived at will point to a particular *Goal-Line* of the traditional *Goal* sequence. An individual that *justifies* their 'wrongness' with "*They are Stupid*" or "*They are Weak*" is obviously operating on the *Goal-Implant,* in these cases, "To Be Intelligent" or "To Be Strong." For example:

--"To Be Intelligent" is a "command-item" that turns *postulate* (as an individual's own *Alpha-Thought*), because it determines the existence of something "*to be*" or "*not be.*"

--The idea that "All Others Are Stupid" is a *consideration,* and an example "*Justification Consideration*" at that; but it is built upon—or added to—the former *postulate.*

I should comment here that when you *process-out* the negative-side of these characteristics, you don't actually lose the positive gains, such as "being intelligent"—you just drop the tendency of using it against people, or having it overshadow your other *Actual* interests and goals. The same is true when we *resurface* and *reduce* other *Imprinting;* we don't lose the *Knowingness* that such-and-such happened, but it no longer has a negative effect on our spiritual well-being.

If the desired computation has resulted from the previous exercises, it may be *analytically inspected,* using PCLs that direct attention toward it "*As-It-Is*"—and of course, this means fully recognizing and understanding its use. Starting with the present life and series of *Goals* and *phases* will ultimately lead into how it sequentially progressed on the *Backtrack,* but it's best to let that data unfold (rather than target it directly) as a *Seeker* increases their *Actualized Awareness*. The following PCLs are used in alternation, but per the Wizard-Level application of upper-routes, the first is applied and run so long as it is still producing answers; then a *Seeker* shifts to the other, runs it, and goes back to the first. This newer style of systematic processing will eventually become second-nature.

a) SPOT ways that ___ would make you *right*.

\ SPOT ways that ___ would make others *wrong*.

b) SPOT ways that ___ would help you *escape domination*.

\ SPOT ways that ___ would help you to *dominate others*.

c) SPOT *ways that* ___ would aid *your survival*.

\ SPOT ways that ___ would hinder the *survival of others*.

Δ Δ Δ Δ Δ Δ

We've already covered, now, how Grade-V picks up where Grade-IV left off. The final subject I want to discuss with you as we close this conference is what part of Grade-V is still in development and will lead directly into Grade-VI. Although this work is all still in development at this time, we have a better certainty now on what we are after and how to get it then we ever did all those years ago when the Systemology Society was first conceived by the alumni of the Mardukite Chamberlains. So, the remaining matter today—as pertinent to the *Backtrack*—is to further clarify the subject of *Implanted-Goals* and *Implanting-Incidents* as they would be most immediately accessible to a Grade-V *Seeker*.

There are multiple *Implanting-Incidents* on the *Backtrack*; those that occur upon entry to a Universe and those that occur more "locally" in-between lifetimes. The same *Implants* have also occurred multiple times; for example, each time an *Alpha-Spirit* had broken free of (or left) *this* Universe, and likely, each time an individual's fixated *genetic-vehicle* expires and they experience death, only to be returned here. There are significant reasons to believe that "after-life" experiences that are reported—and these between-lives "Summerlands"—are all elements of some kind or another of *Implant-Stations.* These exist both figuratively and metaspiritually as "nets" or "screens" or "filters" that trap an *Alpha-Spirit* to *this* "Beta-Existence." *Implants* reinforce the very considerations that keep an *Alpha-Spirit* trapped to these low-level viewpoints and *Games*—those POV that we would typically define as the standard-issue Human Condition.

Keep in mind that in relative contrast to the "*Magic Universe*" immediately preceding this one, this present *Beta-Existence*—what we consider the Physical Universe—is essentially an *Implanted-Penalty Universe* or "prison." Each subsequent condensed Universe began as such from its relatively "higher" and "former" base-line or continuity of existence. Each Universe is a fragmentation of a former fragmented Universe; so, the same descending spiral that is evident on the *Backtrack* is also evident in what each descending Universe is actually made up of as the *Alpha-Spirit* experienced it. This is, of course, where we begin to step onto the grounds of Grade-VI; but where we are concerned with the succession of "*Goals*" and the sequence of an individual's own "*Personality-Phase,*" it is quite relevant to Grade-V.

Since the *Alpha-Spirit* retains its original static position in *Alpha-Existence* and is essentially non-local to any other Universe—except by its own considerations and POV—the shift to lower Universes is generally accomplished with an *Implanting-Incident.* This allows the *Alpha-Spirit* to occupy—and in most cases, be fixated to—a *Beta-Existence* POV, compulsively, continuously and automatically. The *Games*-series of the lower Universe is also *Implanted* upon entrance; it gets added onto the considerations of conditions for the previous Universe, and hence we get further condensation and solidification of Universes. The Game of 'Superiority and Domination' is reinforced upon entrance into this *Beta-Existence*, in addition to the "*Goals-sequence*" by which we assume our various "roles" for supremacy, and failing that, move on to the next *Implanted-Goal* in the sequence—usually the one that stood in opposition the most when we followed the previous "role."

'New Thought' practitioners of previous versions of—and attempts at—"defragmentation" *have* "*spotted*" the *Implanting-Incident* that occurs upon entrance to *this* Universe. Their descriptions of the incident resemble a theatre-style pageant where each of the archetypal "roles" and their associated meanings are *Implanted* with the display of representative characters on the 'stage'. This is meant to introduce an *Alpha-Spirit* to the basic structure of the *Game* upon entering this *Beta-Existence*. This *Imprinting-Incident* is particularly easier to access because it is rooted in '*aesthetics*' rather than coercion and violence. The *Implant* is effective by holding our interest and directing our attention very specifically. The visuals are accompanied by a selective use of "snapping" and "crackling" at specific times—or "angels" blowing trumpets, which in itself, gives a hair-raising insight into what former religions have been running up against.

So, trumpets are blown. The "pageant" of the incident begins with the command-item: "Only One Will Survive." A crowd gathers about the 'stage' as the *Alpha-Spirit* looks on. There may be an impulse to rush the stage, but then comes the line: "To Be The One Who Survives, You Must Be Superior To All Others." A horn sounds. There is a sharp static crackling as the first character appears, who is supposed to be "God." And this may be *spotted* differently by different individuals, though the traditional archetype is the all-too-familiar bearded elderly man in a white robe. The communications continue, but they are not in English and can only be approximated as the "command-items" used in processing.

The "God"-figure instructs the *Alpha-Spirit* (and the apparent 'crowd' gathered, which is likely part of the *Implant* to provide confusion) while looking to his right (your left), stating: "To Be Godlike Is To Solve The Opposition Of Enduring People." Looking forward at everyone, he states: "To Be Godlike Is To Be Superior To All Others." Looking to his left (your right), he says: "To Be Godlike Is To Suffer From The Oppression Of Free Beings." Then, as he exits the stage to your left, from your right, the next character shows up on stage—and it's the "Free Being."

The sequence continues with the "Free Being"-figure addressing everyone. Starting with looking to his right (your left), the direction the "God"-figure exited, he says: "To Be Free Is To Solve The Opposition Of Godlike Beings." Looking forward, he says: "To Be Free Is To Be Superior To All Others." And then to his left, or your right, where the next character is going to come from, he says: "To Be Free Is To Suffer From The Oppression Of Responsible Beings." And then he exits to your left and from your right, the "Responsible Being" comes on stage —and the whole *Implanting-Incident* ensues rather in this pattern through a whole sequence of *Goals* until you end up with 'Enduring Beings', which cycles back to what opposes the "Godlike Being" and everything goes black.

This *Implanting-Incident* is what lays in the "*Goals-sequence*" for "playing" the *Game* of this Universe—and then the *Alpha-Spirit* ends up at an entry-point to this Universe. The entire incident can be "*spotted*" using Grade-V *Piloting* combined with the "Master List of Goal-Sequencing" for this *Beta-Existence*, which I will now give to you here as follows:

To Be Godlike

To Be Free

To Be Responsible

To Be Creative

To Be Important

To Be Competent

To Be Famous

To Be Perceptive

To Be Energetic

To Be Meticulous

To Be Successful

To Be Right (or Accurate)

To Be Popular

To Be Skillful

To Be Wise

To Be Beautiful (or Wanted or Desired)

To Be Productive

To Be Powerful

To Be Holy

To Be Intelligent

To Be Strong

To Be Crafty

To Be Brave

To Be Wealthy

To Be Independent

To Be Good

To Be Adventurous

To Be Orderly

To Be Different

To Be Respected

To Be Happy

To Be Acquisitive

To Be Sensual

To Be Domineering

To Be Tough

To Be Enduring

So, with that "Master List of Goal-Sequencing" in mind, you can easily see how the *Game* of this present Universe has been laid in. And the effect of the *Implant* is held in place by *aesthetics* rather than direct enforcement, so "contacting" or "spotting" this incident is not particularly turbulent on an emotional level; remember, that this is meant to affect our *considerations* and *computations* on the *Game*. But, it also sells you on the idea that to *Play* the *Game* of *this* Universe is "to be superior" and "to be dominant" and thus it directly sets you up to be in *conflict* with everyone else that's also here 'Playing'. But that is part of the whole point: that if you are in *conflict* with everyone else—acting as though you are only operating on the *First Sphere* of existence in exclusion to others—you're going to lose.

For example, a 'Being' in *this* Universe is unable to maintain the "Godlike" *phase*, so eventually everyone sinks into this whole cycle of Goals-sequencing. This represents that proverbial "*Fall*" that we have all experienced—perhaps even more than once, because after we cycle through an entire sequence and end up as "Enduring Beings" we then begin the cycle again, to a lesser degree or as a lesser version of the "Godlike" state, and the declining spiral perpetuates further. The only direct example I can give is my own, where several thousand years have been spent in a transition from the *Goal* "To Be Holy" toward "To Be Intelligent"—and I guess that's where you end up with a '*Nabu*-cult' of '*priest-scribes*', but that's a longer story than we have time for now.

Needless to say, a Grade-V *Seeker* should be in a position to arrange the data we have covered this weekend into a workable regimen for their own practices; which should suffice until we can prepare a more proper supplemental "workbook" for Wizard Level-1. And to break free of these *Implanted* patterns for this *Game*, we must first stop fighting our fellows in this artificial position of superiority. The fundamental fragmentation that is directly implanted leads to the notion that "there can be *only one*"—"that *only one* will survive" and this is untrue. It does, however, keep the *Games* going down here—and that is the only purpose for it. Once we *realize* it '*As-It-Is*', we can change our course, change our *postulates*, turn around, and go back the way we descended; because obviously *this* is not where we want to be.

The *Implanting-Incident* concerning 'Entering This Universe' is a useful one to know about because it is the *first* incident of its type pertaining to this *Beta-Existence*, and one that is likely to have been restimulated and built-upon in subsequent, more recent, *Implanting-Incidents*. This means that as a *Seeker* explores more of this type of material in Grade-V—and their own exploration of the *Backtrack*—if at any point the handling of another more turbulent *Implanting-Incident* becomes too overwhelming, you can actually "cool-off" the session by "*spotting*" that first *Implanting-Incident* for *this* Universe. It doesn't actually "discharge" or "disentangle" the more recent *Implants*, like you find with *Imprints* on a chain, but it does aid in preserving the gains achieved up to that point, if suddenly a *Seeker* is overwhelmed. So, this should all assist you in *processing* your way out of *this Game*.

Years ago, we realized that 'The Way Out' would systematically resemble the routes by which we descended. We understood that the 'Gates' reflected in our most archaic esoteric lore were pointing toward a realization that had been lost in translation along the way—and that our only hope of finding a Map to this Pathway was in recovering that lost understanding. I believe that our Systemology has successfully delivered a communication that is unparalleled into today's society, and most of you can attest that above and beyond the former gradients of knowledge available to us in our world, this work we are doing now is our best chance at "making the grade" to reach our Ascension in this lifetime—and for the first time in a very long time, reclaim the true power of the Alpha-Spirit and the freedom to experience an existence of its own true Self-determined creation. We are making great strides on the Pathway now, and I'm so pleased there are those of you here that are with us now as we do this. Together we will dream up a better world; and together we will make it happen. Thank you for offering your presence here with us this weekend. I hope some of what we've discussed will be of benefit to you on your journey. Good night.

TO BE GODLIKE — TO BE FREE
TO BE RESPONSIBLE — TO BE CREATIVE
TO BE IMPORTANT — TO BE COMPETENT
TO BE FAMOUS — TO BE PERCEPTIVE
TO BE ENERGETIC — TO BE METICULOUS
TO BE SUCCESSFUL — TO BE ACCURATE
TO BE POPULAR — TO BE SKILLFUL
TO BE WISE — TO BE WANTED
TO BE PRODUCTIVE — TO BE POWERFUL
TO BE HOLY — TO BE INTELLIGENT
TO BE STRONG — TO BE CRAFTY
TO BE BRAVE — TO BE WEALTHY
TO BE INDEPENDENT — TO BE GOOD
TO BE ADVENTUROUS — TO BE ORDERLY
TO BE DIFFERENT — TO BE RESPECTED
TO BE HAPPY — TO BE ACQUISITIVE
TO BE SENSUAL — TO BE DOMINEERING
TO BE TOUGH — TO BE ENDURING
TO BE GODLIKE

.: APPENDIX :.
GAMES-SERIES UNIVERSE IMPLANTS
PLATFORM CROSS-LIST
(ADAPTED FROM "LIBER-3E")

Sphere 8:	To Enlighten
	To Convert
	To Commune
	To Worship
Sphere 7:	To Predict
	To Influence
	To Protect
	To Embody
Sphere 6:	To Discover
	To Locate
	To Gather
	To Own
Sphere 5:	To Grow
	To Experience
	To Heal
	To Adapt
Sphere 4:	To Establish
	To Share
	To Control
	To Unite
Sphere 3:	To Organize
	To Cooperate
	To Participate
	To Expand
Sphere 2:	To Join
	To Reproduce
	To Enjoy
	To Protect
Sphere 1:	To Feel
	To Eat
	To Survive
	To Endure

158

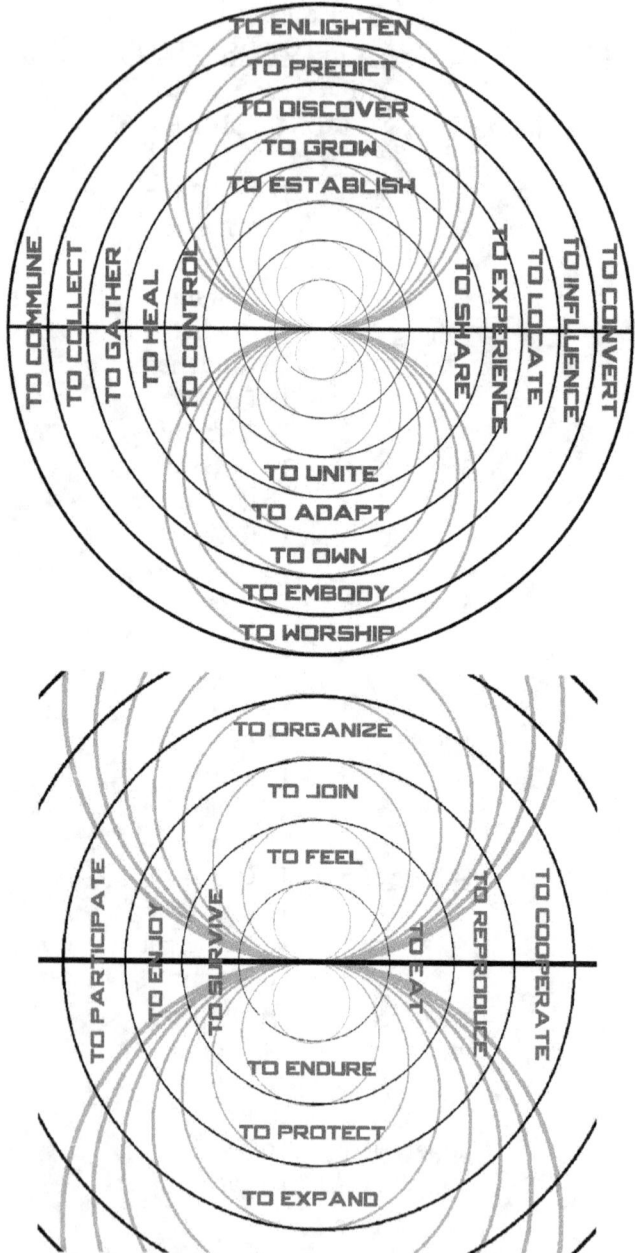

THE SYSTEMOLOGY
BACKTRACK
TECHNICAL DICTIONARY

SYSTEMOLOGY BACKTRACK GLOSSARY

A-for-A (one-to-one) : an expression meaning that what we say, write, represent, think or symbolize is a direct and perfect reflection or duplication of the actual aspect or thing—that "A" is for, means and is equivalent to "A" and not "a" or "q" or "!"; in the relay of communication, the message or particle is sent and perfectly duplicated in form and meaning when received.

acknowledgment : a response-communication establishing that an immediately former communication was properly received, duplicated and understood; the formal acceptance and/or recognition of a communication or presence.

activating event (restimulation) : an incident or occurrence that automatically stimulates a conscious or unrecognized reminder or 'ping' from an earlier *imprinting incident* recorded on one's own personal timeline as an emotionally charged and encoded memory; an incident or instance when thought systems are activated to determine the consequence or significance of an activity, motion or event—often demonstrated as *Activating Event → Belief Systems → Consideration.*

actualization : to make actual, not just potential; to bring into full solid Reality; to realize fully in *Awareness* as a "thing."

affinity : the apparent and energetic *relationship* between substances or bodies; the degree of *attraction* or repulsion between things based on natural forces; the *similitude* of frequencies or waveforms; the degree of *interconnection* between systems.

agreement (reality) : unanimity of opinion of what is "thought" to be known; an accepted arrangement of how things are; things we consider as "real" or as an "is" of "reality"; a consensus of what is real as made by standard-issue (common) participants; what an individual contributes to or accepts as "real"; in *NexGen Systemology*, a synonym for *"reality."*

allegorical : a representation of the abstract, metaphysical or "spiritual" using physical or concrete forms.

alpha : the first, primary, basic, superior or beginning of some form; in *NexGen Systemology*, referring to the state of existence operating on spiritual archetypes and postulates, will and intention "exterior" to the low-level condensation and solidarity of energy and matter as the 'physical universe'.

alpha control center (ACC) : the highest relay point of *Beingness* for an individuated *Alpha-Spirit, Self* or "I-AM"; in *NexGen Systemology*—a point of spiritual separation of ZU at (7.0) from the *Infinity of Nothingness* (8.0); the truest actualization of *Identity*; the highest *Self-directed* relay of *Alpha-Self* as an *Identity-Continuum*, operating in an *Alpha-Existence* (or "Spiritual Universe"–AN) to *determine* "Alpha Thought" (6.0) and WILL-*Intention* (5.0) *exterior* to the "Physical Universe"–(KI); the "wave-peak" of "I" emerging as individuated consciousness from *Infinity*.

alpha-spirit : a "spiritual" *Life*-form; the "true" *Self* or I-AM; the *individual*; the spiritual (*alpha*) *Self* that is animating the (*beta*) physical body or "*genetic vehicle*" using a continuous *Lifeline* of spiritual ("*ZU*") energy; an individual spiritual (*alpha*) entity possessing no physical mass or measurable waveform (motion) in the Physical Universe as itself, so it animates the (*beta*) physical body or "*genetic vehicle*" as a catalyst to experience *Self*-determined causality in effect within the *Physical Universe*; a singular unit or point of *Spiritual Awareness* that is *Aware* that it is *Aware*.

alpha thought : the highest spiritual *Self-determination* over creation and existence exercised by an Alpha-Spirit; the Alpha range of pure *Creative Ability* based on direct postulates and considerations of *Beingness*; spiritual qualities comparable to "thought" but originating in Alpha-existence (at "6.0") independently superior to a *beta-anchored* Mind-System, although an Alpha-Spirit may use Will ("5.0") to carry the intentions of a postulate or consideration ("6.0") to the Master Control Center ("4.0").

AN : an ancient "Sumerian" cuneiform sign for Heaven or "God"; in *Mardukite Zuism and Systemology* designating the '*spiritual zone*' (or '*Alpha Existence*'); the *Spiritual Universe*— comprised of spiritual matter and spiritual energy; a direction of motion toward spiritual *Infinity*, away from or superior to the physical (*'KI'*); the spiritual condition of existence providing for our primary *Alpha* state as an individual *Identity* or *I-AM-Self* which interacts and experiences *Awareness* of a *beta* state in the *Physical Universe* (*'KI'*) as *Life*.

Ancient Mystery School : the original arcane source of all esoteric knowledge on Earth, concentrated between the Middle East and modern-day Turkey and Transylvania c. 6000 B.C. and then dispersing south (Mesopotamia), west (Europe) and east (Asia) from that location.

apparent : visibly exposed to sight; evident rather than actual, as presumed by Observation; readily perceived, especially by the senses.

archetype : a "first form" or ideal conceptual model of some aspect; the ultimate prototype of a form on which all other conceptions are based.

ascension : actualized *Awareness* elevated to the point of true "spiritual existence" exterior to *beta existence*. An "Ascended Master" is one who has returned to an incarnation on Earth as an inherently *Enlightened One*, demonstrable in their actions —they have the ability to *Self-direct* the "Spirit" as *Self*, just as we are treating the "Mind" and "Body" at this current grade of instruction; previously treated in *Moroii ad Vitam* as a state of Beingness after *First Death*, experienced by an *etheric body*, which is able to maintain consciousness as a personal identity continuum with the same *Self-directed* control and communication of Will-Intention that is exercised, actualized and developed deliberately during one's present incarnation.

associative knowledge : significance or meaning of a facet or aspect assigned to (or considered to have) a direct relationship with another facet; to connect or relate ideas or facets of existence with one another; a reactive-response image, emotion or conception that is suggested by (or directly accompanies) something other than itself; in traditional systems logic, an equivalency of significance or meaning between facets or sets that are grouped together, such as in *(a + b) + c = a + (b + c)*; in NexGen Systemology, erroneous associative knowledge is assignment of the same value to all facets or parts considered as related (even when they are not actually so), such as in $a = a$, $b = a$, $c = a$ and so forth without distinction.

assumption : the act of taking or gathering to one's Self; taking possession of, receive or behold.

attention : active use of *Awareness* toward a specific aspect or thing; the act of "attending" with the presence of *Self*; a direction of focus or concentration of *Awareness* along a particular channel or conduit or toward a particular terminal node or communication termination point; the Self-directed concentration of personal energy as a combination of observation, thought-waves and consideration; focused application of *Self-Directed Awareness*.

authoritarian : knowledge as truth, boundaries and freedoms dictated to an individual by a perceived, regulated or enforced "authority."

awareness : the highest sense of-and-as Self in knowing and being as I-AM (the *Alpha-Spirit*); the extent of beingness directed as a POV experienced by Self as knowingness.

axiom : a fundamental truism of a knowledge system, esp. *logic*; all *maxims* are also *axioms*; knowledge statements that require no proof because their truth is self-evident; an established law or systematic principle used as a *premise* on which to base greater conclusions of truth.

Babylonian : the ancient Mesopotamian civilization that evolved from *Sumer*; inception point for systematization of civic society and religion.

Back-Scan : to apply Awareness, *Zu-Vision* or "Alpha-Sight" (*exterior* to the *Human Condition*) and *resurface* impressions for recreating *Mental Imagery* of the *Backtrack* within one's own Personal Universe and treat with Wizard-Level (*Grade-V+*) methodology.

Backtrack : to retrace one's steps or go back to an early point in a sequence; an applied spiritual philosophy within *Metahuman Systemology "Wizard Grades"* regarding continuous existence of an individual's "*Spiritual Timeline*" through all lifetime-incarnations; the course that is already laid behind us; a methodology of systematic processing methods developed to assist in revealing "hidden" *Mental Images* and *Imprints* from one's past and reclaim attention-energies "left behind" with them by increasing ability to manage and control personal energy mechanisms fixed to their continuous automated creation.

band : a division or group; in *NexGen Systemology*, a division or set of frequencies on the ZU-line that are tuned closely together and referred to as a group.

BAT (Beta-Awareness Test) : a method of *psychometric evaluation* developed for *Mardukite Systemology* to determine a "basic" or "average" state of personal *beta-Awareness*; first developed for the text *"Crystal Clear."*

beta (awareness) : all consciousness activity (*"Awareness"*) in the "Physical Universe" (KI) or else *beta-existence*; *Awareness* within the range of the *genetic-body*, including material thoughts, emotional responses and physical motors; personal *Awareness* of physical energy and physical matter moving through physical space and experienced as "time"; the *Awareness* held by *Self* that is restricted to a physical organic *Lifeform* or *"genetic vehicle"* in which it experiences causality in the *Physical Universe*.

beta (existence) : all manifestation in the "Physical Universe" (KI); the "Physical" state of existence consisting of vibrations of physical energy and physical matter moving through physical space and experienced as "time"; the conditions of *Awareness* for the *Alpha-spirit* (*Self*) as a physical organic *Lifeform* or *"genetic vehicle"* in which it experiences causality in the *Physical Universe*.

beta-defragmentation : toward a state of *Self-Honesty* in regards to handling experience of the "Physical Universe" (*beta-existence*); an applied spiritual philosophy (or technology) of Self-Actualization originally described in the text *"Crystal Clear"* (*Liber-2B*), building upon theories from *"Systemology: The Original Thesis."*

biological unconsciousness : the organism independent of the sentient *Awareness* of the *Self* to direct it; states induced by severe injury and anesthesia.

biomagnetic/biofeedback : a measurable effect, such as a change in electrical resistance, that is produced by thoughts, emotions and physical behaviors which generate specific 'neurotransmitters' and biochemical reactions in the brain, body and across the skin surface.

capable : the actual capacity for potential ability.

CAT (Creative Ability Training) : a method of increasing personal freedom and unlimited creative potential of the Alpha-Spirit (Self) independent and exterior to conditions and reality agreements with beta-existence; a Wizard-Level training regimen first developed for the Grade-IV text *"Imaginomicon"* (*Liber-3D*).

catharsis / cathartic processing : from the Greek root meaning "pure" or "perfect"; Gnostic practices of "consolamentum" where an individual removes distorting/fragmented emotional charges and encoding from a personal energy flow/circuit connected or associated with some terminal, mass, thing, *&tc.*; in *NexGen Systemology*, the emptying out or discharge of emotional stores; also *"abreaction"* or *"Route-1."*

causative : as being the cause; to be at cause.

channel : a specific stream, course, current, direction or route; to form or cut a groove or ridge or otherwise guide along a specific course; a direct path; an artificial aqueduct created to connect two water bodies or water or make travel possible.

charge : to fill or furnish with a quality; to supply with energy; to lay a command upon; in *NexGen Systemology*—to imbue with intention; to overspread with emotion; application of *Self-directed (WILL)* "intention" toward an emotional manifestation in beta-existence; personal energy stores and significances entwined as fragmentation in mental images, reactive-response encoding and intellectual (and/or) programmed beliefs; in traditional mysticism, to intentionally fix an energetic resonance to meet some degree, or to bring a specific concentration of energy that is transferred to a focal point, such as an object or space.

circuit : a circular path or loop; a closed-path within a system that allows a flow; a pattern or action or wave movement that follows a specific route or potential path only; in *NexGen Systemology*, *"communication processing"* pertaining to a specific flow of energy or information along a channel; *see* also *"feedback loop."*

chronologically : concerning or pertaining to "time"; to treat as "units" of "time" ; to sequence a series of events or information with regard to the order it happened or originated (in time).

codification : process of collecting, analyzing and then arranging knowledge in a standardized and more accessible systematic form, often by subject, theme or some other designation.

collapsing a wave : also, *"wave-function collapse"*; in *Quantum Physics*, the concept that an Observer is "collapsing" the wave-function to something "definite" by measuring it; defining or calculating a wave-function or interaction of potential interactions by an Observation; in *NexGen Systemology*, when a wave of potentiality or possibility because a finite fixed form; Consciousness or *Awareness* "collapses" a wave-function of energy-matter as a necessary "third" Principle of Apparent Manifestation (first described in *"Tablets of Destiny"*); potentiality as a wave is collapsed into an apparent *"is"*, the energy of which is freed up in systematic processing by *"flattening"* a "collapsed" wave back into its state of potentiality.

command : in *Metahuman Systemology*, responsibility and ability of Self (I-AM) as operating from its ideal "exterior" *Point-of-View* as Alpha Spirit; to direct communication for control of the *genetic vehicle* and Mind-Body connection that is perfectly duplicated from a source-point to a receipt-point along the ZU-line.

command line : see *"processing command line"* (PCL).

communication : successful transmission of information, data, energy (&tc.) along a message line, with a reception of feedback; an energetic flow of intention to cause an effect (or duplication) at a distance; the personal energy moved or acted upon by will or else 'selective directed attention'; the 'messenger action' used to transmit and receive energy across a medium; also relay of energy, a message or signal—or even locating a personal POV (viewpoint) for the Self—along the *ZU-line*.

compulsion : a failure to be responsible for the dynamics of *command* and *control*—starting, stopping or altering—on a particular channel of communication and/or regarding a particular terminal in existence; an energetic flow with the appearance of being 'stuck' on the action it is already doing or by the control of some automatic mechanism.

concept : a high-frequency thought-wave representing an "idea" which persists because it is not restricted to a unique space-time; an abstract or tangible "idea" formed in the "Mind" or *imagined* as a means of understanding, usually including associated "Mental Images"; a seemingly timeless collective thought-theme (or subject) that entangles together facets of many events or incidents, not just a single significant one.

conceptual processing : a Wizard-Level methodology introduced intermittently throughout materials of Metahuman Systemology that emphasizes fully "getting the sense of" (or "contacting the idea of") a particular condition as prompted by a PCL and on one's own determination; a systematic practice-drill regarding considerations and postulates (Alpha Thought) regarding various reality agreements; a *Route-0* variant employing *Creativeness* and *Imagination* for systematic processing; also *Route-0E* when used for *Ethics Processing.*

condense (condensation) : the transition of vapor to liquid; denoting a change in state to a more substantial or solid condition; leading to a more compact or solid form.

condition : an apparent or existing state; circumstances, situations and variable dynamics affecting the order and function of a system; a series of interconnected requirements, barriers and allowances that must be met; in "contemporary language," bringing a thing toward a specific, desired or intentional new state (such as in "conditioning"), though to minimize confusion about the word "condition" in our literature, *NexGen Sys-*

temology treats "contemporary conditioning" concepts as imprinting, encoding and programming.

conflict : the opposition of two forces of similar magnitude along the same channel or competing for the same terminal; the inability to duplicate another POV; a thought, intention or communication that is met with an opposing counter-thought or counter-intention that generates an energetic cluster.

confront : to come around in front of; to be in the presence of; to stand in front of, or in the face of; to meet "face-to-face" or "face-up-to"; additionally, in *NexGen Systemology*, to fully tolerate or acceptably withstand an encounter with a particular manifestation or encounter.

consciousness : the energetic flow of *Awareness*; the Principle System of *Awareness* that is spiritual in nature, which demonstrates potential interaction with all degrees of the Physical Universe; the *Beingness* component of our existence in *Spirit*; the Principle System of *Awareness* as *Spirit* that directs action in the Mind-System.

consensual (consensus) : formed or existing simply by consent—by general or mutual agreement; permitted, approved or agreed upon by majority of opinion; knowingly agreed upon unanimously by all concerned; to be in agreement on the objective universe and/or a course of action therein.

consideration : careful analytical reflection of all aspects; deliberation; determining the significance of a "thing" in relation to similarity or dissimilarity to other "things"; evaluation of facts and importance of certain facts; thorough examination of all aspects related to, or important for, making a decision; the analysis of consequences and estimation of significance when making decisions; in *NexGen Systemology*, the postulate or Alpha-Thought that defines the state of beingness for what something "*is.*"

continuity : being a continuous whole; a complete whole or "total round of"; the balance of the equation ["–120" + "120" = "0" &*tc*.]; an apparent unbroken interconnected coherent whole; also, as applied to Universes in *NexGen Systemology*, the lowest base consideration of space-time or commonly shared level of energy-matter apparent in an existence, or else the lowest degree of solidity or condensation whereby all mass that exists is identifiable or communicable with all other mass that exists; represented as "0" on the *Standard Model* for the Physical Universe (*beta-existence*), a level of existence that is below Human emotion, comparable to the solidity of "rocks" and "walls" and "inert bodies."

continuum : a continuous enduring uninterrupted sequence or condition; observing all gradients on a *spectrum*; measuring quantitative variation with gradual transition on a spectrum without demonstrating discontinuity or separate parts.

control (general) : the ability to start, change or start some action or flow of energy; the capacity to originate, change or stop some mode of human behavior by some implication, physical or psychological means to ensure compliance (voluntarily or involuntarily).

control (systems) : communication relayed from an operative center or organizational cluster, which incites new activity elsewhere in a system (or along the *ZU-line*).

correlate : a relationship between two or more aspects, parts or systems.

correspondence : a direct relationship or correlation; see also *"associative knowledge."*

Cosmic History : the entire continuous *Spiritual Timeline* or *Backtrack* of all existence, starting with the *Infinity of Nothingness* and individuation of Self and its Home Universe, running through various Games Universes and ultimately leading to condensation and solidification of this Physical Universe experienced in present-time.

creative ability test : see *"CAT."*

creativeness processing : a *systematic processing* methodology introduced in *Grade-IV Metahuman Systemology* (*Wizard Level-0*) that emphasizes personal use of *"Imagination,"* or else "creative ability" of Self and freeing considerations of the Alpha-Spirit to *Be* or *Create* anything within its Personal Universe, independent of reality agreements with beta-existence;

also "*Route-0.*"

Crystal Clear : the second professional publication of Mardukite Systemology, released publicly in December 2019; the second professional text in Grade-III Mardukite Systemology, released as "*Liber-2B*" and reissued in the Grade-III Master Edition "*Systemology Handbook*"; contains fundamental theory of "*Beta-Defragmentation*" and "*Route-2*" systematic processing methodology.

cuneiform : the oldest extant writing system at the inception of modern civilization in Mesopotamia; a system of wedge-shaped script inscribed on clay tablets with a reed pen, allowing advancements in record keeping and communication no longer restricted to more literal graphic representations or pictures.

dead-memories : outdated, inadequate or erroneous data.

defragmentation : the *reparation* of wholeness; collecting all dispersed parts to reform an original whole; a process of removing "*fragmentation*" in data or knowledge to provide a clear understanding; applying techniques and processes that promote a *holistic* interconnected *alpha* state, favoring observational *Awareness* of continuity in all spiritual and physical systems; in *NexGen Systemology*, a "*Seeker*" achieving an actualized state of basic "*Self-Honest Awareness*" is said to be *beta-defragmented*, whereas *Alpha-defragmentation* is the rehabilitation of the *creative ability*, managing the *Spiritual Timeline* and the POV of *Self* as Alpha-Spirit (I-AM); see also "*Beta-defragmentation.*"

degree : a physical or conceptual *unit* (or point) defining the variation present relative to a *scale* above and below it; any stage or extent to which something *is* in relation to other possible positions within a *set* of "*parameters*"; a point within a specific range or spectrum; in *NexGen Systemology*, a *Seeker's* potential energy variations or fluctuations in thought, emotional reaction and physical perception are all treated as "*degrees.*"

dichotomy : a division into two parts, types or kinds.

differential : the quantitative value difference between two forces, motions, pressures or degrees.

differentiation : an apparent difference between aspects or concepts.

discernment : to perceive, distinguish and/or differentiate experience into true knowledge.

dogma : religious doctrines or opinion-based beliefs (data-set) treated socially as fact, especially regarding "divinity" or "God" (the common "Human" interpretation of the "domain" of Infinity) represented by the "Eighth Sphere" on our original Standard Model of Systemology; religiously defined values, taboos and ethical standards emphasized by cultural/religious socialization and mythographic beliefs (even above any observable causal effects, logical sequences or verifiable proofs).

dramatization / dramatize : a vivid display or performance as if rehearsed for a "play" (on stage); a *'circuit'* recording *'imprinted'* in the past and, once restimulated by a facet of the environment, the individual "replays" it as through reacting to it in the present (and identifying that reality as present reality); acts, actions and observable behaviors that demonstrate identification with a particular character type, "phase" or personality program; a motivated sequence-chain, implant series or imprinted cycle of actions—usually irrational or counter-survival —repeated by an individual as it had previously happened to them; a reoccurring or reactively triggered out-flow, communication or action that indicates an individual "occupying" a particular *'Point-of-View'* (*POV*)—typically fixed to a specific (past) identification (identity) that is space-time locatable (meaning a point where significant *attention-energy*—enough to compulsively create and maintain a POV—is "stuck" or "hung up" on the *BackTrack*).

Eastern traditions : the evolution of the *Ancient Mystery School* east of its origins, primarily the Asian continent, or what is archaically referred to as "oriental."

emotional encoding : the readable substance/material (data) of *'imprints'*; associations of sensory experience with an *imprint*; perceptions of our environment that receive an *emotional charge*, which form or reinforce facets of an *imprint*; perceptions recorded and stored as an *imprint* within the "emotional range" of energetic manifestation; the formation of an energetic store or charge on a channel that fixes emotional responses as a mechanistic automation, which is carried on in an individual's *Spiritual Timeline* (or personal continuum of existence).

end-point : the moment when the goal of a process has been achieved and to continue on with it will be detrimental to the gains; the finality of a process when the *Seeker* has achieved their optimum state from the current cycle (whether or not they run through it again at a later date with a different level of *Awareness* or knowledge base doesn't change the fact that it has flattened the standing *collapsed* wave-form).

enforcement : the act of compelling or putting (effort) into force; to compel or impose obedience by force; to impress strongly with applications of stress to demand agreement or validation; the lowest-level of direct control by physical effort or threat of punishment; a low-level method of control in the absence of true communication.

entanglement : tangled together; intertwined and enmeshed systems; in *NexGen Systemology*, a reference to the interrelation of all particles as waves at a higher point of connectivity than is apparent, since wave-functions only "collapse" when someone is *Observing*, or doing the measuring, evaluating, &tc.

epicenter : the point which shock-waves travel from.

esoteric : hidden; secret; knowledge understood by a select few.

ethics : an intellectual philosophy concerning *rightness* and *wrongness* based on "logic" and "reason" (rationale) combined with observable consequences and tendencies of action or conduct; formal name for a "moral philosophy" (study of moral choices); in ancient times, originally treated *one-to-one* with "Cosmic Law" regarding *causation, order* and *sequence*; an objective (Universal) philosophy of *rightness* and *wrongness*, treated separate from culture-specific (subjective/relative) considerations, such as *morals* and *dogma*; in *NexGen Systemology* (*Grade-IV Metahuman Systemology*), a dynamic philosophy (applying "logic-and-reason") to understand the nature of "reality agreements" concerning *rightness* and *wrongness*, then treating the most optimum conditions of continued existence ("SURVIVAL" in *Beta-existence*; "CREATION" in *Alpha*) for the highest affected "Sphere of Existence" (on the *Standard Model*).

ethics processing : a *systematic processing* methodology introduced for bridging *Grade-IV Metahuman Systemology (Wizard Level-0)* with *Grade-V Spiritual Systemology (Wizard Level-1)* that emphasizes personal realization of *"Ethics"* and increased ability and responsibility to confront the "rightness" and "wrongness" of past actions (on the Backtrack), including defragmentation of *"Harmful Acts"* (as *Imprinting Incidents*) and any corresponding *"Hold-Backs"* and *"Hold-Outs"* (which reduce *Actualized Awareness* and prompt an individual to *withdraw* their *reach*); also *"Route-3E."*

evaluate : to determine, assign or fix a set value, amount or meaning.

existence : the *state* or fact of *apparent manifestation*; the resulting combination of the Principles of Manifestation: consciousness, motion and substance; continued *survival*; that which independently exists; the *'Prime Directive'* and sole purpose of all manifestation or Reality; the highest common intended motivation driving any *"Thing"* or *Life*.

existential : pertaining to existence, or some aspect or condition of existence.

experiential data : accumulated reference points we store as memory concerning our "experience" with Reality.

extant : in existence; existing.

exterior : outside of; on the outside; in *NexGen Systemology*, we mean specifically the POV of *Self* that is *'outside of'* the *Human Condition,* free of the physical and mental trappings of the Physical Universe; a metahuman range of consideration; see also *'Zu-Vision'*.

facets : an aspect, an apparent phase; one of many faces of something; a cut surface on a gem or crystal; in *NexGen Sys-*

temology—a single perception or aspect of a memory or *"Imprint"*; any one of many ways in which a memory is recorded; perceptions associated with a painful emotional (sensation) experience and *"imprinted"* onto a metaphoric lens through which to view future similar experiences; other secondary terminals that are associated with a particular terminal, painful event or experience of loss, and which may exhibit the same encoded significance as the activating event.

faculties : abilities of the mind (individual) inherent or developed.

feedback loop : a complete and continuous circuit flow of energy or information directed as an output from a source to a target which is altered and return back to the source as an input; in *General Systemology*—the continuous process where outputs of a system are routed back as inputs to complete a circuit or loop, which may be closed or connected to other systems/circuits; in *NexGen Systemology*—the continuous process where directed *Life* energy and *Awareness* is sent back to *Self* as experience, understanding and memory to complete an energetic circuit as a loop.

flattening a wave : see *"process-out"* for definition; also see *"collapsing a wave."*

flow : movement across (or through) a channel (or conduit); a direction of active energetic motion typically distinguished as either an *in-flow*, *out-flow* or *cross-flow*, defined as *"circuits"* in processing.

fragmentation : breaking into parts and scattering the pieces; the *fractioning* of wholeness or the *fracture* of a holistic interconnected *alpha* state, favoring observational *Awareness* of perceived connectivity between parts; *discontinuity*; separation of a totality into parts; in *NexGen Systemology*, a person outside a state of *Self-Honesty* is said to be *fragmented*.

game : a strategic situation where a "player's" power of choice is employed or affected; a parameter or condition defined by purposes, freedoms and barriers (rules).

game theory : a mathematical theory of logic pertaining to strategies of maximizing gains and minimizing loses within prescribed boundaries and freedoms; a field of knowledge widely applied to human problem solving and decision-making; the application of true knowledge and logic to deduce the correct course of action given all variables and interplay of dynamic systems; logical study of decision making where "players" make choices that affect (the interests) of other "players"; an intellectual study of conflict and cooperation.

genetic memory : the evolutionary, cellular and genetic (DNA) "memory" encoded into a *genetic vehicle* or *living organism* during its progression and duplication (reproduction) over millions (or billions) of years on Earth; in *NexGen Systemology*—the past-life Earth-memory carried in the genetic makeup of an organism (*genetic vehicle*) that is *independent of any* actual "spiritual memory" maintained by the *Alpha Spirit* themselves, from its own previous lifetimes on Earth and elsewhere using other *genetic vehicles* with no direct evolutionary connection to the current physical form in use.

genetic-vehicle : a physical *Life*-form; the physical (*beta*) body that is animated/controlled by the (*Alpha*) *Spirit* using a continuous *Lifeline* (ZU); a physical (*beta*) organic receptacle and catalyst for the (*Alpha*) *Self* to operate "causes" and experience "effects" within the *Physical Universe*.

gradient : a degree of partitioned ascent or descent along some scale, elevation or incline; "higher" and "lower" values in relation to one another.

GSR-Meter ("galvanic skin response"–"electropsychometer") : a *biofeedback* device used for measuring electrical resistance (in "Ohms") of the skin surface; one of many parts used in a polygraph system; a highly sensitive "Ohm-meter" with variable range, set points and amplification used to monitor electrical fluctuations of the skin surface.

harmful-act : a counter-survival mode of behavior or action (esp. that causes harm to one of more *Spheres of Existence*)— or—an overtly aggressive (hostile and/or destructive) action against an individual or any other *Sphere of Existence*; in *Utilitarian Systemology*—a shortsighted (serves fewest/lowest *Spheres of Existence*) intentional overtly harmful action to resolve a perceived problem; a revision of the rule for standard *Utilitarianism* for Systemology to distinguish actions which provide the least benefit to the least number of *Spheres of Existence*, or else the greatest harm to the greatest number of *Spheres of Existence*; in *moral philosophy*—an action which can be experienced by few and/or which one would not be willing to experience for themselves (*theft, slander, rape, &tc*); an iniquity or iniquitous act.

help : to assist survival of; aid continuing optimum success.

hold-back : withheld communications (esp. actions) such as "*Hold-Outs*"; intentional (or automatic) withdrawal (as opposed to reach); Self-restraint (which may eventually be enforced or automated); not reaching, acting or expressing, when one should be; an ability that is now restrained (on automatic) due to inability to withhold it on Self-determinism alone.

hold-outs : in photography, the numerous snapshots/pictures withheld from the final display or professional presentation of the event; withheld communications; in Utilitarian Systemology—energetic withdrawal and communication breaks with a "*terminal*" and its *Sphere of Existence* as a result of a "*Harmful-Act*"; unspoken or undiscovered (hidden, covert) actions that an individual withholds communications of, fearing punishment or endangerment of *Self-preservation* (*First Sphere*); the act of hiding (or keeping hidden) the truth of a "*Harmful-Act*"; a refusal to communicate with a *Pilot*; also "*Hold-Back.*"

Homo Novus : literally, the "new man"; the "newly elevated man" or "known man" in ancient Rome; the man who "knows (only) through himself"; in NexGen Systemology—the next spiritual and intellectual evolution of *homo sapiens* (the "modern Human Condition"), which is signified by a demonstration of higher faculties of *Self-Actualization* and clear *Awareness*.

Homo Sapiens Sapiens : the present standard-issue Human Condition; the *hominid* species and genetic-line on Earth that received modification, programming and conditioning by the *Anunnaki* race of *Alpha-Spirits*, of which early alterations contributed to various upgrades (changes) to the genetic-line, beginning approximately 450,000 years ago (*ya*) when the *Anunnaki* first appear on Earth; a species for the Human Condition on Earth that resulted from many specific *Anunnaki* "genetic" and "cultural" *interventions* at certain points of significant advancement—specifically (but not limited to) *circa* 300,000 *ya*, 200,000 *ya*, 40,000 *ya,* and 8,000 *ya*; a species of the Human Condition set for replacement by *Homo Novus*.

hot button : something that triggers or incites an intense emotional reaction instantaneously; in *NexGen Systemology*—a slang term denoting a highly reactive *channel*, heavily *charged* with a long chain of cumulative *emotional imprinting*, typically (but not necessarily) connected to a significant or "primary" *implant*; a non-technical label, first applied during *Grade-IV Professional Piloting "Flight School"* research sessions of Spring-Summer 2020, to indicate specific circuits, channels or terminals that cause a *Seeker* to immediately react with intense emotional responses, whether in general, directed to the *Pilot*, or even at effectiveness of processing.

Human Condition : a standard default state of Human experience that is generally accepted to be the extent of its potential identity (*beingness*)—currently treated as *Homo Sapiens Sapiens,* but which is scheduled for replacement by *Homo Novus*.

identification : the association of *identity* to a thing; a label or fixed data-set associated to what a thing is; association "equals" a thing, the "equals" being key; an equality of all things in a group, for example, an "apple" identified with all other "apples"; the reduction of "I-AM"-*Self* from a *Spiritual Beingness* to an "identity" of some form.

identity : the collection of energy and matter—including memory—across a "*Spiritual Timeline*" that we consider as "I" of *Self*, but the "I" is an individual and not an identification with anything other than *Self* as *Alpha-Spirit*.

identity-system : the application of the *ZU-line* as "I"—the continuous expression of *Self* as *Awareness* across a "*Spiritual Timeline*"; see "*identity*."

imagination : the ability to create *mental imagery* in one's Personal Universe at will and change or alter it as desired; the ability to create, change and dissolve mental images on command or as an act of will; to create a mental image or have associated imagery displayed (or "conjured") in the mind that may or may not be treated as real (or memory recall) and may or may not accurately duplicate objective reality; to employ *Creative Abilities* of the Spirit that are independent of reality agreements with beta-existence.

Imaginomicon : the fourth professional publication of Mardukite Systemology, released publicly in mid- 2021; the second professional text in Grade-IV Metahuman Systemology, released as *"Liber-3D"*; contains fundamental theory of *"Spiritual Ability"* and *"Route-0"* systematic processing methodology.

imperative : a high-level authoritarian command; a command triggering urgency and necessity of a certain goal or directive; see also *"Spheres of Existence"* and *"Prime Directive."*

implant : to graft or surgically insert; to establish firmly by setting into; to instill or install a direct command or consideration in consciousness (Mind-System, &tc.); a mechanical device inserted beneath the surface/skin; in *Metahuman Systemology*, an "energetic mechanism" (linked to an Alpha-Spirit) composing a circuit-network and systematic array of energetic receptors underlying and filter-screening communication channels between the Mind-System and *Self*; an energetic construct installed upon entry of a Universe; similar to a platen or matrix or circuit-board, where each part records a specific type or quality of *emotionally encoded imprints* and other "heavily charged" *Mental Images* that are "impressed" by future encounters; a basic platform on which certain *imprints* and *Mental Images* are encoded (keyed-in) and stored (often beneath the surface of "knowing" or *Awareness* for that individual, although an implanted "command" toward certain inclinations or behavioral tendencies may be visibly observable.

imprint : to strongly impress, stamp, mark (or outline) onto a softer 'impressible' substance; to mark with pressure onto a surface; in *NexGen Systemology*, the term is used to indicate permanent Reality impressions marked by frequencies, energies or interactions experienced during periods of emotional

distress, pain, unconsciousness, loss, enforcement, or something antagonistic to physical (personal) survival, all of which
are are stored with other reactive response-mechanisms at
lower-levels of *Awareness* as opposed to the active memory
database and proactive processing center of the Mind; an experiential "memory-set" that may later resurface—be triggered
or stimulated artificially—as Reality, of which similar responses will be engaged automatically; holographic-like imagery "stamped" onto consciousness as composed of energetic
facets tied to the "snap-shot" of an experience.

imprinting incident : the first or original event instance communicated and *emotionally encoded* onto an individual's "*Spiritual Timeline*" (recorded memory from all lifetimes), which
formed a permanent impression that is later used to mechanist-
ically treat future contact on that channel; the first or original
occurrence of some particular *facet* or mental image related to
a certain type of *encoded response*, such as pain and discomfort, losses and victimization, and even the acts that we have
taken against others along the Spiritual Timeline of our existence that caused them to also be *Imprinted*.

incarnation : a present, living or concrete form of some thing,
idea or beingness; an individual lifetime or life-cycle from
birth/creation to death/destruction independent of other lifetimes or cycles.

inception : the beginning, start, origin or outset.

incite : to urge on or cause; instigate; prove or stimulate into
action.

individual : a person, lifeform, human entity or creature; a
Seeker or potential *Seeker* is often referred to as an "individual" within Mardukite Zuism and Systemology materials.

inhibited : withheld, held-back, discouraged or repressed from
some state.

"in phase" : see "*phase alignment.*"

insistence : repeated use of a communicated energy into a
form that demands acknowledgment, is more difficult to avoid
or ignore.

intention : the directed application of Will; to intend (have "in Mind") or signify (give "significance" to) for or toward a particular purpose; in *NexGen Systemology* (from the *Standard Model*)—the spiritual activity at WILL (5.0) directed by an *Alpha Spirit* (7.0); the application of WILL as "Cause" from a higher order of Alpha Thought and consideration (6.0), which then may continue to relay communications as an "effect" in the universe.

inter-dimensional : systems that are interconnected or correlated between the Physical Universe and the Spiritual Universe —or between "dimension states" observably identified as "physical," "emotional," "psychological" and "spiritual." The only point of true interconnectivity that we can systematically determine is called "*Life*" or the POV of *Self.*

intermediate : a distinct point between two points; actions or relay between two points.

internal : a force coming from inside; information received from inside sources; in *NexGen Systemology*, the objective *'Physical Universe'* experience of *beta-existence* that is associated with the Physical Body or *genetic vehicle* and its POV regarding sensation and perception; from inside the body; within the body.

invalidate : decrease the level or degree or *agreement* as Reality.

invest : spend on; give or devote something in exchange for a beneficial result; to endow with.

knowledge : clear personal processing of informed understanding; information (data) that is actualized as effectively workable understanding; a demonstrable understanding on which we may 'set' our *Awareness*—or literally a "knowledge."

KI : an ancient cuneiform sign designating the *'physical zone'*; the *Physical Universe*—comprised of physical matter and physical energy in action across space and observed as time; a direction of motion toward material *Continuity*, away from or subordinate to the Spiritual (*'AN'*); the physical condition of existence providing for our *beta* state of *Awareness* experienced (and interacted with) as an individual *Lifeform* from our primary Alpha state of Identity or *I-AM-Self* in the *Spiritual Universe ('AN')*.

level : a physical or conceptual *tier* (or plane) relative to a *scale* above and below it; a significant *gradient* observable as a *foundation* (or surface) built upon and subsequent to other levels of a totality or whole; a *set* of "*parameters*" with respect to other such *sets* along a *continuum*; in *NexGen Systemology*, a *Seeker's* understanding, *Awareness* as *Self* and the formal grades of material/instruction are all treated as "*levels*."

Liber-One : First published in October 2019 as "*The Tablets of Destiny: Using Ancient Wisdom to Unlock Human Potential*" by Joshua Free; republished in the complete *Grade-III* antho-logy, "*The Systemology Handbook*"; revised in August 2022 as "*The Tablets of Destiny (Revelation): How Long-Lost Anun-naki Wisdom Can Change the Fate of Humanity.*"

Liber-Two : First published in October 2020 as "*Metahuman Destinations: Piloting the Course to Homo Novus*" by Joshua Free; an anthology of the *Grade-IV* "Professional Piloting Course," containing revised materials from *Liber-2C*, *Liber-2D* and (most of) *Liber-3C*; republished in the complete *Grade-IV* anthology, "*The Metahuman Systemology Hand-book*"; republished as two volumes in 2022.

Liber-Three : see "*Liber-3E.*"

Liber-2B : First published in December 2019 as "*Crystal Clear: The Self-Actualization Manual & Guide to Total Awareness*" by Joshua Free; republished in the complete *Grade-III* anthology, "*The Systemology Handbook*"; revised in April 2022 as "*Crystal Clear (Handbook for Seekers): Achieve Self-Actualization and Spiritual Ascension in This Lifetime.*"

Liber-2C : First published in April 2020 as "*Communication and Control of Energy & Power: The Magic of Will & Inten-tion (Volume One)*" by Joshua Free; revision republished as an integral part of the *Grade-IV* "Professional Piloting Course," in October 2020 within "*Metahuman Destinations*" (*Liber-Two*); republished in the complete *Grade-IV* anthology, "*The Metahuman Systemology Handbook.*"

Liber-2D : First published in June 2020 as *"Command of the Mind-Body Connection: The Magic of Will & Intention" (Volume Two)"* by Joshua Free; revision republished as an integral part of the *Grade-IV* "Professional Piloting Course," in October 2020 within *"Metahuman Destinations"* (*Liber-Two*); republished in the complete *Grade-IV* anthology, *"The Metahuman Systemology Handbook."*

Liber-3C : First published in July 2020 as *"Now You Know: The Truth About Universes & How You Got Stuck in One"* by Joshua Free; a discourse in the *Grade-IV* Metahuman Systemology series; a revision of one part republished in October 2020 within the *"Professional Piloting Course"* manual, *"Metahuman Destinations"* (*Liber-Two*), a revision of the remaining part republished in June 2021 within the *"Imaginomicon"* (*Liber-3D*); republished in the complete *Grade-IV* anthology, *"The Metahuman Systemology Handbook."*

Liber-3D : First published in June 2021 as *"Imaginomicon: The Gateway to Higher Universes (A Grimoire for the Human Spirit)"* by Joshua Free; a manual completing the *Grade-IV* (Metahuman Systemology) professional series with a treatment of "Wizard Level-0"; revised in June 2022 as *"Imaginomicon (Revised Edition): Approaching Gateways to Higher Universes (A New Grimoire for the Human Spirit)"*; republished in the complete *Grade-IV* anthology, *"The Metahuman Systemology Handbook."*

Liber-3E (Liber-Three) : First published in April 2022 as *"The Way of the Wizard: Utilitarian Systemology (A New Metahuman Ethic)"* by Joshua Free; a professional manual bridging *Grade-IV* (Metahuman Systemology, *Wizard Level-0*) with *Grade-V* (Spiritual Systemology, *Wizard Level-1*); republished in the complete *Grade-IV* anthology, *"The Metahuman Systemology Handbook."*

localized : brought together and confined to a particular place.

logic : philosophical science of correct *reasoning*.

macrocosmic : taking examples and system demonstrations at one level and applying them as a larger demonstration of a relatively higher level or unseen dimension.

manifestation : something brought into existence.

Marduk : founder of Babylonia; patron Anunnaki "god" of Babylon.

Mardukite Zuism : a Mesopotamian-themed (Babylonian-oriented) religious philosophy and tradition applying the spiritual technology based on *Arcane Tablets* in combination with "Tech" from *NexGen Systemology*; first developed in the New Age underground by Joshua Free in 2008 and realized publicly in 2009 with the formal establishment of the *Mardukite Chamberlains.* The text *"Tablets of Destiny"* is a cross-over from Mardukite Zuism (and Mesopotamian Neopaganism) toward higher spiritual applications of Systemology.

Master-Control-Center (MCC) : a perfect computing device to the extent of the information received from "lower levels" of sensory experience/perception; the proactive communication system of the *"Mind"*; a relay point of active *Awareness* along the Identity's *ZU-line*, which is responsible for maintaining basic *Self-Honest Clarity* of *Knowingness* as a *seat of consciousness* between the *Alpha-Spirit* and the secondary *"Reactive Control Center"* of a *Lifeform* in *beta existence*; the Mind-center for an *Alpha-Spirit* to actualize cause in the *beta existence*; the analytical *Self-Determined* Mind-center of an *Alpha-Spirit used* to project *Will* toward the genetic body; the point of contact between *Spiritual Systems* and the *beta existence*; presumably the *"Third Eye"* of a being connected directly to the *I-AM-Self*, which is responsible for *determining* Reality at any time; in *NexGen Systemology*, this is plotted at (4.0) on the continuity model of the *ZU-line*.

MCC : see *"Master-Control-Center."*

mental image : a subjectively experienced "picture" created and imagined into being by the Alpha-Spirit (or at lower levels, one of its automated mechanisms) that includes all perceptible *facets* of totally immersive scene, which may be forms originated by an individual, or a "facsimile-copy" ("snapshot") of something seen or encountered; a duplication of wave-forms in one's Personal Universe as a "picture" that mirror an "external" Universe experience, such as an *Imprint*.

Mesopotamia : land between Tigris and Euphrates River; modern-day Iraq; the primary setting for ancient *Sumerian* and *Babylonian* traditions thousands of years ago, including activities and records of the *Anunnaki*.

metahumanism : an applied philosophy of *transhumanism* with an emphasis on "spiritual technologies" as opposed to "external" ones; a new state or evolution of the *Human Condition* achievable on planet Earth, rooted in *Self-Honesty*, whereby individuals are operating *exterior* to considerations that are fixed exclusively to the *genetic vehicle* (Human Body) and independent of the *emotional encoding* and *associative programming* typical of the present standard-issue *Human Condition*.

Metahuman Destinations : the third professional publication of Mardukite Systemology, released publicly in October 2020; the first professional text in Grade-IV Metahuman Systemology, released as "*Liber-Two*" and containing materials from *Liber-2C, Liber-2D* and *Liber-3C*; contains fundamental theory of "*Professional Piloting*" and "*Route-3*" systematic processing methodology.

meter : a device used to measure; see *GSR-Meter*.

methodology : a complete system of applications, methods, principles and rules to compose a *'systematic'* paradigm as a "whole"—esp. a field of philosophy or science.

misappropriated : put into use incorrectly; to apply ineffectively or as unintended by design or definition.

morals : widely held culturally conditioned (socially learned) ethical standards of conduct used to "judge" *rightness* from *wrongness* of an individual's character, personality or actions (which may or may not be intellectually and emotionally influenced by "local" religious customs, taboos and *dogma*; basic social reality agreements determining "proper conduct" and "right actions" (behavior) based on civic *laws*, social *codes* and religious *doctrines* of a particular society or group and its own cultural experiences of *Reality*.

Nabu : the *Anunnaki* "god of wisdom, writing and knowledge" for Babylonian (Mardukite) Tradition.

negligible : so small or trifle that it may be disregarded.

NexGen Systemology : a modern tradition of applied religious philosophy and spiritual technology based on *Arcane Tablets* in combination with *"general systemology"* and *"games theory"* developed in the New Age underground by Joshua Free in 2011 as an advanced futurist extension of the *"Mardukite Chamberlains"*; also referred to as *"Mardukite Systemology,"* *"Metahuman Systemology"* and *"Spiritual Systemology."*

objective : concerning the "external world" and attempts to observe Reality independent of personal "subjective" factors.

one-to-one : see *"A-for-A."*

organic : as related to a physically living organism or carbon-based life form; energy-matter condensed into form as a focus or POV of Spiritual Life Energy (*ZU*) as it pertains to beta-existence of *this* Physical Universe (*KI*).

paradigm : an all-encompassing *standard* by which to view the world and *communicate* Reality; a standard model of reality-systems used by the Mind to filter, organize and interpret experience of Reality.

parameters : a defined range of possible variables within a model, spectrum or continuum; the extent of communicable reach capable within a system or across a distance; the defined or imposed limitations placed on a system or the functions within a system; the extent to which a Life or "thing" can *be*, *do* or *know* along any channel within the confines of a specific system or spectrum of existence.

participation : being part of the action; contributing control or effort; affecting the result.

patterns (probability patterns) : observation of cycles and tendencies to predict a causal relationship or determine the actual condition or flow of dynamic energy using a holistic systemology to understand Life, Reality and Existence as opposed to isolating or excluding perceived parts as being mutually separate from other perceived parts.

PCL : see *"processing command line."*

perception : internalized processing of data received by the *senses*; to become *Aware of* via the senses.

personality (program, phase) : the total composite picture an individual "identifies" themselves with; the accumulated sum of material and mental mass by which an individual experiences as their timeline; a "beta-personality" is mainly attached to the identity of a particular physical body and the total sum of its own genetic memory in combination with the data stores and pictures maintained by the Alpha Spirit; a "true personality" is the Alpha Spirit as Self completely defragmented of all erroneous limitations and barriers to consideration, belief, manifestation and intention.

phase (identification) : in *NexGen Systemology,* a pattern of personality or identity that is assumed as the POV from *Self*; personal identification with artificial "personality packages"; an individual assuming or taking characteristics of another individual (often unknowingly as a response-mechanisms); also "*phase alignment.*"

phase alignment or "*in phase*" : to be in synch or mutually synchronized, in step or aligned properly with something else in order to increase the total strength value; in *NexGen Systemology*, alignment or adjustment of *Awareness* with a particular identity, space or time; perfect *defragmentation* would mean being "in phase" as *Self* fully conscious and Aware as an Alpha-Spirit *in* present *space* and *time,* free of synthetic personalities.

pilot : a professional steersman responsible for healthy functional operation of a ship toward a specific destination; in *NexGen Systemology*, an intensive trained individual qualified to specially apply *Systemology Processing* to assist other *Seekers* on the *Pathway.*

ping : a short, high pitched ring, chime or noise that alerts to the presence of something; in computer systems, a query sent on a network or line to another terminal in order to determine if there is a connection to it; in *NexGen Systemology*, the sudden somatic twinge or pain or discomfort that is felt as a sensation in the body when a particular terminal (lifeform, object, concept) is 'brought to mind' or contacted on a personal communication channel-circuit; the accompanying sensations and mental images that are experienced as an automatic-response to the presence of some channel or terminal.

player (game theory) : an individual that is making decisions in a game and/or is affected by decisions others are making in the game, especially if those other-determined decisions now affect the possible choices.

point-of-view (POV) : a point to view from; an opinion or attitude as expressed from a specific identity-phase; a specific standpoint or vantage-point; a definitive manner of consideration specific to an individual phase or identity; a place or position affording a specific view or vantage; circumstances and programming of an individual that is conducive to a particular response, consideration or belief-set (paradigm); a position (consideration) or place (location) that provides a specific view or perspective (subjective) on experience (of the objective).

postulate : to put forward as truth; to suggest or assume an existence *to be*; to state or affirm the existence of particular conditions; to provide a basis of reasoning and belief; a basic theory accepted as fact; in *NexGen Systemology*, "Alpha-Thought"—the top-most decisions or considerations made by the Alpha-Spirit regarding the *"is-ness"* (what things "are") about energy-matter and space-time.

potentiality : the total "sum" (collective amount) of "latent" (dormant—present but not apparent) capable or possible realizations; used to describe a state or condition of what has not yet manifested, but which can be influenced and predicted based on observed patterns and, if referring to beta-existence, Cosmic Law.

POV : see *"point-of-view"* and/or *"POV Processing."*

POV processing : a methodology of *Grade-IV Metahuman Systemology* emphasizing systematic processing toward realizations that improve a Seeker's willingness to manage a present POV and associated *phases*, their ability to transfer POVs freely, increased tolerance to experiences (or encounters) with any other viewpoint, and finally, an actualized realization that a POV is not one-to-one with *Beingness* of *Self*; an extension of *creativeness processing* and "Wizard Level" training that systematically handles *Awareness* of "points" and "spots" in space, from which an Alpha-Spirit may place its own viewpoint of a dimension or Universe—also a prerequisite to upper-route practices such as "*Zu-Vision*" and "*Backtrack.*"

premise : a basis or statement of fact from which conclusions are drawn.

presence : the quality of some thing (energy/matter) being "present" in space-time; personal orientation of *Self* as an *Awareness* (*POV*) located in present space-time (environment) and communicating with extant energy-matter.

prevalent : of wide extent; an extensive or largely accepted aspect or current state.

probability : the causal likelihood for something to result, "effect" or manifest in and as a certain way, manner or degree, based on "observed evaluation" of programming and tendencies that follow Cosmic Law.

"process-out" or **"flatten a wave"** : to reduce *emotional encoding* of an *imprint* to zero; to dissolve a *wave-form* or *thought-formed* "solid" such as a "*belief*"; to completely run a *process* to its end, thereby *flattening* any previously "*collapsed-waves*" or *fragmentation* that is obstructing the *clear channel* of *Self-Awareness*; also referred to as "processing-out"; to discharge all previously held emotionally encoded imprinting or erroneous programming and beliefs that otherwise fix the free flow (wave) to a particular pattern, solid or concrete "*is*" form.

processing, systematic : the inner-workings or "through-put" result of systems; in *NexGen Systemology*, a methodology of applied spiritual technology used toward personal Self-Actualization; methods of selective directed attention, communicated language and associative imagery that targets an increase in personal control of the human condition.

processing command line (PCL) or **command line** : a directed input; a specific command using highly selective language for *Systemology Processing*; a predetermined directive statement (cause) intended to focus concentrated attention (effect).

projecting awareness : sending out (motion) or radiating "*consciousness*" from *Self* ("I") to another POV.

proportional : having a direct relationship or mutual interaction with.

protest : a response-communication objecting an enforcement or a rejection of a prior communication; an effort to cancel, re-write or destroy the existence or "is-ness" (what something "is") of a previous creation or communication; unwillingness to be the Point-of-View of effect or (receipt-point) for a communication.

rationality / reasoning (game theory) : the extent to which a player seeks to play (make decisions, &tc.) in order to maximize the gains (or else survival) achievable within any given game conditions; the ability and willingness of an individual to reach toward conditions that promote the highest level of survival and existence and make the best choices and moves to see the desired goal manifest.

reactive control center (RCC) : the secondary (reactive) communication system of the "*Mind*"; a relay point of *Awareness* along the Identity's *ZU-line*, which is responsible for engaging basic motors, biochemical processes and any *programmed automated responses* of a living *beta* organism; the reactive Mind-Center of a living organism relaying communications of *Awareness* between causal experience of *Physical Systems* and the "*Master Control Center*"; it presumably stores all emotional encoded imprints as fragmentation of "chakra" frequencies of *ZU* (within the range of the "*psychological/emotive systems*" of a being), which it may *react* to as Reality at any time; in *NexGen Systemology*, this is plotted at (2.0) on the continuity model of the *ZU-line*.

reality : see "*agreement.*"

realization : the clear perception of an understanding; a consideration or understanding on what is "actual"; to make "real" or give "reality" to so as to grant a property of "beingness" or "being as it is"; the state or instance of coming to an *Awareness*; in *NexGen Systemology*, "gnosis" or true knowledge achieved during *systematic processing*; achievement of a new (or "higher") cognition, true knowledge or perception of Self; a consideration of reality or assignment of meaning.

relative : an apparent point, state or condition treated as distinct from others.

religion : a concise spiritual *paradigm*, set of beliefs and practices regarding "Divinity," "Infinite Beingness"—or else, "God"—as representative symbol of the *Eighth Sphere of Existence* for *Beta-Existence* (or else "Infinity").

repetitively : to repeat "over and over" again; or else "repetition."

responsibility : the *ability* to *respond*; the extent of mobilizing *power* and *understanding* an individual maintains as *Awareness* to enact *change*; the proactive ability to *Self-direct* and make decisions independent of an outside authority.

restimulation : see *"activating event."*

resurface : to return to (or bring up to) the "surface" of that which has previously been submerged; in *NexGen Systemology*—relating specifically to processes where a *Seeker* recalls blocked energy stored covertly as emotional *"imprints"* (by the RCC) so that it may be effectively defragmented from the *"ZU-line"* (by the MCC).

Route-0 : a specific methodology from *SOP-2C* denoting *"Creativeness Processing,"* as described in the text *"Imaginomicon"* (*Liber-3D*).

Route-0E : a specific methodology (expanding on *Route-0* from *Liber-3D*) denoting *"Conceptual Processing"* applied to *Ethics Beta-Defragmentation*, as described in the text *"Way of the Wizard"* (*Liber-Three* or *Liber-3E*).

Route-1 : a specific methodology from *SOP-2C* denoting *"Resurfacing Processing,"* as described in the text *"Tablets of Destiny"* (*Liber-One*) as "RR-SP" (and reissued in *"The Systemology Handbook"*).

Route-2 : a specific methodology from *SOP-2C* denoting *"Analytical-Recall Processing,"* as described in the text *"Crys-*

tal Clear" (*Liber-2B*) as "AR-SP" (and reissued in *"The Systemology Handbook"*).

Route-3 : a specific methodology from *SOP-2C* denoting *"Communication-Circuit Processing,"* as described in the text *"Metahuman Destinations"* (*Liber-Two*); also the basis for *SOP-2C* routine.

Route-3E : a specific methodology (expanding on *Route-3* from *SOP-2C*) denoting *"Ethics Processing,"* as described in the text *"The Way of the Wizard"* (*Liber-Three* or *Liber-3E*); also related to "Standard Procedure R-3E."

Seeker : an individual on the *Pathway to Self-Honesty*; a practitioner of *Mardukite Systemology* or *NexGen Systemology Processing* that is working toward *Spiritual Ascension*.

Self-actualization : bringing the full potential of the Human spirit into Reality; expressing full capabilities and creativeness of the *Alpha-Spirit*.

Self-determinism : the freedom to act, clear of external control or influence; the personal control of Will to direct intention.

Self-honesty : the basic or original *alpha* state of *being* and *knowing*; clear and present total *Awareness* of-and-as *Self*, in its most basic and true proactive expression of itself as *Spirit* or *I-AM*—free of artificial attachments, perceptive filters and other emotionally-reactive or mentally-conditioned programming imposed on the human condition by the systematized physical world; the ability to experience existence without judgment.

semantics : the *meaning* carried in *language* as the *truth* of a "thing" represented, *A-for-A*; the *effect* of language on *thought* activity in the Mind and physical behavior; language as *symbols* used to represent a concept, "thing" or "solid."

sensation : an external stimulus received by internal sense organs (receptors/sensors); sense impressions.

sine-wave : the *frequency* and amplitude of a quantified (calculable) *vibration* represented on a graph (graphically) as smooth repetitive *oscillation* of a *waveform*; a *waveform* graphed for demonstration—otherwise represented in *NexGen Systemology* logic equations as 'W*f*,' or in mathematics as the *'function of x'* (*fx*); graphically representing arcs (*parameters*) of a circular *continuity* on a *continuum*; in the *Standard Model of NexGen Systemology*, the actual 'wave vibration' graphically displayed on an otherwise static *ZU-line* (of Infinity) is a *'sine-wave'.*

slate : a hard thin flat surface material used for writing on; a chalk-board, which is a large version of the original wood-framed writing slate, named for the rock-type it was made from.

SOP-2C : *Standard Operating Procedure #2C* or *Systemology Operating Procedure #2C*; a standardized procedural formula introduced in materials for *"Metahuman Destinations"* (*Liber-Two*); a regimen or outline for standard delivery of systematic processing used by *Systemology Pilots* and *Mardukite Ministers*; a procedure outline of systematic processing, which includes applications of *"Route-1," "Route-2," "Route-3"* and *"Route-0"* as taught for *Grade-IV Professional Piloting*.

space : a viewpoint or *Point-of-View* (POV) extended from any point out toward a dimension or dimensions; the consideration of a point or spot as an *anchor* or *corner* in addition to others, which collectively define parameters of a dimensional plane; the field of energy/matter mass created as a result of communication and control in action and measured as time (wave-length), such as "distance" between points (or peaks on a wave).

spectrum : a broad range or array as a continuous series or sequence; defined parts along a singular continuum; in physics, a gradient arrangement of visible colored bands diffracted in order of their respective wavelengths, such as when passing *White Light* through a *prism*.

Spheres of Existence (dynamic systems) : a series of *eight* concentric circles, rings or spheres (each larger than the former) that is overlaid onto the Standard Model of Beta-Existence to demonstrate the dynamic systems of existence extending out from the POV of Self (often as a "body") at the *First*

Sphere; these are given in the basic eightfold systems as: *Self, Home/Family, Groups, Humanity, Life on Earth, Physical Universe, Spiritual Universe* and *Infinity-Divinity.*

spiritual timeline : a continuous stream of moment-to-moment *Mental Images* (or a record of experiences) that defines the "past" of a spiritual being (or *Alpha-Spirit*) and which includes impressions (*imprints, &tc.*) form all life-incarnations and significant spiritual events the being has encountered; in NexGen Systemology, also "*backtrack.*"

standard issue : equally dispensed to all.

standard model : a fundamental *structure* or symbolic construct used to evaluate a complete *set* in *continuity* relative to itself and variable to all other *dynamic systems* as graphed or calculated by *logic*.

Standard Model, The (systemology) : in *NexGen Systemology*—our existential and cosmological *standard model* or cabbalistic model; a "*monistic continuity model*" demonstrating *total system* interconnectivity "above" and "below" observation of any apparent *parameters*; the original presentation of the *ZU-line*, represented as a singular vertical (y-axis) waveform in space across dimensional levels or Universes (*Spheres of Existence*) without charting any specific movement across a dimensional time-graph x-axis; The Standard Model of Systemology represents the basic workable synthesis of common denominators in models explored throughout Grade-I and Grade-II material.

static : characterized by a fixed or stationary condition; having no apparent change, movement or fluctuation.

successively : what comes after; forward into the future.

superstition : knowledge accepted without good reason.

symbol : a concentrated mass with associated meaning or significance.

system : from the Greek, "to set together"; to set or arrange things or data together so as to form an orderly understanding of a "whole"; also a *'method'* or *'methodology'* as an orderly standard of use or application of such data arranged together.

systematization : to arrange into systems; to systematize or make systematic.

Systemology : see *"NexGen Systemology."*

Systemology Procedure 1-8-0 : advanced spiritual technology within our Systemology, which applies a methodology of systematic practice for experiencing: (1) Self-Awareness, (8) Nothingness and (0) Beingness, introduced for "Crystal Clear" but expanded on for *"Imaginomicon"*; *'one-eight-zero'* is included in, but not the same as application *'one-eighty'*—or else the *Beta-Defrag-Intensive* called *"SOP-180"* or *"Systemology-180."*

Systemology-180 : an intensive systematic processing routine employing all *Grade-III, Grade-IV* and cross-over *Wizard-Level* work to date; the total sum of all effective philosophical and spiritual applications necessary to professionally *Pilot* a *Seeker* to reach a stable point of *Self-Honesty* and basic *Beta-Defragmentation*, as a prerequisite to treating *"Actualized-Ascension Technologies"* (*A.T.*) of upper-level *Wizard Grades*; a textbook released in 2023.

Tablets of Destiny : the first professional publication of Mardukite Systemology, released publicly in October 2019; the first professional text in Grade-III Mardukite Systemology, released as *"Liber-One"* and reissued in the Grade-III Master Edition *"Systemology Handbook"*; contains fundamental theory of the *"Standard Model"* and *"Route-1"* systematic processing methodology.

terminal (node) : a point, end or mass on a line; a point or connection for closing an electric circuit, such as a post on a battery terminating at each end of its own systematic function; any end point or 'termination' on a line; a point of connectivity with other points; in systems, any point which may be treated as a contact point of interaction; anything that may be distinguished as an 'is' and is therefore a 'termination point' of a system or along a flow-line which may interact with other related systems it shares a line with; a point of interaction with other points; an "energetic-mass" or *noun* defragmented with systematic processing.

thought-form : apparent *manifestation* or existential *realization* of *Thought-waves* as "solids" even when only apparent in Reality-agreements of the Observer; the treatment of *Thought-waves* as permanent *imprints* obscuring *Self-Honest Clarity* of *Awareness* when reinforced by emotional experience as actualized "thought-formed solids" ("*beliefs*") in the Mind; energetic patterns that "surround" the individual.

thought-wave or **wave-form** : a proactive *Self-directed action* or reactive-response *action* of *consciousness*; the *process* of *thinking* as demonstrated in *wave-form*; the *activity* of *Awareness* within the range of *thought vibrations/frequencies* on the existential *Life-continuum* or *ZU-line*.

threshold : a doorway, gate or entrance point; the degree to which something is to produce an effect within a certain state or condition; the point in which a condition changes from one to the next.

tier : a series of rows or levels, one stacked immediately before or atop another.

time : observation of cycles in action; motion of a particle, energy or wave across space; intervals of action related to other intervals of action as observed in Awareness; a measurable wave-length or frequency in comparison to a static state; the consideration of variations in space.

timeline : plotting out history in a linear (line) model to indicate instances (experiences) or demonstrate changes in state (space) as measured over time; a singular conception of continuation of observed time as marked by event-intervals and changes in energy and matter across space.

transhumanism : a social science and applied philosophy concerning the next evolved state of the "*Human Condition*,"; progress in two potential directions, either "spiritual" technologies advancing *Self* as an "Alpha-Spirit," or the direction of "external"-"physical" technologies that modify or eliminate characteristics of the *Body*; a theme describing contemporary application of material sciences emphasizing only "physical" and "genetic" parts of the *Human* experience, such as brain activity, cell-life extension and space travel; *NexGen Systemo-*

logy recently began distinguishing its emphasis on "spiritual technology" as *"metahumanism."*

traumatic encoding : information received when the sensory faculties of an organism are "shocked" into learning it as an "emotionally" encoded *Imprint*; a duplicated facsimile-copy or *Mental Image* of severe misfortune, violent threats, pain and coercion, which is then categorized, stored and reactively retrieved based exclusively on its emotional *facets.*

treat / treatment : an act, manner or method of handling or dealing with someone, something or some type of situation; to apply a specific process, procedure or mode of action toward some person, thing or subject; use of a specific substance, regimen or procedure to make an existing condition less severe; also, a written presentation that handles a subject in a specific manner.

turbulence : a quality or state of distortion or disturbance that creates irregularity of a flow or pattern; the quality or state of aberration on a line (such as ragged edges) or the emotional "turbulent feelings" attached to a particular flow or terminal node; a violent, haphazard or disharmonious commotion (such as in the ebb of gusts and lulls of wind action).

unconscious : a state when *Awareness* as *Self* is removed totally from the equation of *Life* experience, though it continues to be recorded in lower-level response mechanisms (fixed to a simulacrum or genetic vehicle) for later retrieval.

undefiled : to remain intact, untouched or unchanged; to be left in an original "virgin" state.

understanding : a clear '*A-for-A*' duplication of a communication as 'knowledge', which may be comprehended and retained with its significance assigned in relation to other 'knowledge' treated as a 'significant understanding'; the "grade" or "level" that a knowledge base is collected and the manner in which the data is organized and evaluated.

validation : reinforcement of agreements or considerations as "real."

vibration : effects of motion or wave-frequency as applied to any system.

viewpoint : see *"point-of-view" (POV)*.

wave-form : see *"sine-wave."*

wave-function collapse : see *"collapsing a wave."*

will *or* **WILL** (5.0) : in *NexGen Systemology* (from the *Standard Model*), the Alpha-ability at "5.0" of a Spiritual Being (*Alpha Spirit*) at "7.0" to apply *intention* as "Cause" from consideration or Alpha-Thought at "6.0" that is superior to "beta-thoughts" that only manifest as reactive "effects" below "4.0" and *interior* to the *Human Condition*.

willingness : the state of conscious Self-determined ability and interest (directed attention) to *Be*, *Do* or *Have*; a Self-determined consideration to reach, face up to (*confront*) or manage some "mass" or energy; the extent to which an individual considers themselves able to participate, act or communicate along some line, to put attention or intention on the line, or to produce (create) an effect.

ZU : the ancient Sumerian cuneiform sign for the archaic verb —*"to know," "knowingness"* or *"awareness"*; in *Mardukite Zuism and Systemology*, the active energy/matter of the "Spiritual Universe" (AN) experienced as a *Lifeforce* or *consciousness* that imbues living forms extant in the "Physical Universe" (KI); *"Spiritual Life Energy"*; energy demonstrated by the WILL of an actualized *Alpha-Spirit* in the "Spiritual Universe" (AN), which impinges its *Awareness* into the Physical Universe (KI), animating/controlling *Life* for its experience of *beta-existence* along an individual Alpha-Spirit's personal *Identity-continuum*, called a *ZU-line*.

Zu-**Line** : a theoretical construct in *Mardukite Zuism and Systemology* demonstrating *Spiritual Life Energy* (ZU) as a personal individual "continuum" of Awareness interacting with all Spheres of Existence on the Standard Model of Systemology; a spectrum of potential variations and interactions of a monistic continuum or singular *Spiritual Life Energy (ZU)* demonstrated on the Standard Model; an energetic channel of potential POV and "locations" of Beingness, demonstrated in early Systemology materials as an individual Alpha-Spirit's personal *Iden* *tity-continuum*, potentially connecting *Awareness (ZU)* of *Self* with "*Infinity*" simultaneous with all points considered in existence; a symbolic demonstration of the "*Life-line*" on which *Awareness (ZU)* extends from the direction of the "Spiritual Universe" (AN) in its true original *alpha state* through an entire possible range of activity resulting in its *beta state* and control of a *genetic-entity* occupying the *Physical Universe (KI)*.

Zu-Vision : the true and basic (*Alpha*) Point-of-View (perspective, POV) maintained by *Self* as *Alpha-Spirit* outside boundaries or considerations of the *Human Condition* "Mind-Systems" and *exterior* to beta-existence reality agreements with the Physical Universe; a POV of Self *as* "a unit of Spiritual Awareness" that exists independent of a "body" and entrapment in a *Human Condition*; "spirit vision" in its truest sense.

WOULD YOU LIKE
TO KNOW
MORE
?

SYSTEMOLOGY
The Pathway to Self-Honesty

A Basic Introduction to Mardukite Systemology

THE WAY INTO THE FUTURE

A Handbook for the New Human

a collection of
writings by
Joshua Free
selected by
James Thomas

Here are the basic answers to what has held Humanity back from achieving its ultimate goals and unlocking the true power of the Spirit and highest state of Knowing and Being.

"The Way Into The Future" illuminates the *Pathway* leading to Planet Earth's true "metahuman" destiny. With <u>excerpts</u> from *"Tablets of Destiny," "Crystal Clear," "Systemology—The Original Thesis"* and *"The Power of Zu."* You can help shine clear light on anyone's pathway!

Carefully selected by Mardukite Publications Officer, James Thomas, this critical *collection of eighteen articles, lecture transcripts and reference chapters* by Joshua Free is sure to be not only a treasured part of your personal library, but also the perfect introduction for all friends, family and loved ones.

(Basic Grade-III Introductory Pocket Anthology)

SYSTEMOLOGY

The Pathway to Self-Honesty

ORIGINAL UNDERGROUND INTRODUCTIONS
REVISED AND REISSUED IN HARDCOVER

SYSTEMOLOGY

The Original Thesis of Mardukite New Thuoght

by Joshua Free

(*Mardukite Systemology Liber-S-1X*)

The very first underground discourses released to the "New Thought" division of the Mardukite Research Organization privately over a decade ago and providing the inspiration for rapid futurist spiritual technology called "Mardukite Systemology."

THE POWER OF ZU

Applying Mardukite Zuism & Systemology to Everyday Life

by Joshua Free
Foreword by Reed Penn

(*Mardukite Systemology Liber-S-1Z*)

A unique introductory course on Mardukite Zuism & Systemology, including transcripts from a 3-day lecture series given by Joshua Free in December 2019 to launch the Mardukite Academy of Systemology & Founding Church of Mardukite Zuism just in time for the 2020's.

SYSTEMOLOGY
The Pathway to Self-Honesty

THE TABLETS OF DESTINY REVELATION

How Long-Lost Anunnaki Wisdom Can Change the Fate of Humanity

by Joshua Free

Mardukite Systemology Liber-One

second edition

Discover the origins of the Pathway to Self-Honesty with the book that started it all!

In this newly revised "Revelations" Academy Edition: Rediscover the original system of perfecting the Human Condition on a Pathway that leads to Infinity. Here is a way!—a map to chart spiritual potential and redefine the future of what is means to be human.

A landmark public debut for Grade-III Systemology and the foundation stone for reaching higher and taking back control of your DESTINY!

The revelation of 6,000 year old secrets, providing the tools and wisdom to unlock human potential...

SYSTEMOLOGY
The Pathway to Self-Honesty

CRYSTAL CLEAR
Handbook for Seekers

Achieving
Self-Actualization
& Spiritual Ascension
in This Lifetime

by Joshua Free

Mardukite Systemology
Liber-2B

second edition

Take control of your destiny and chart the first steps toward your own spiritual evolution.

Realize new potentials of the Human Condition with a Self-guiding handbook for Self-Processing toward Self-Actualization in Self-Honesty using actual techniques and training provided for the coveted "Mardukite Self-Defragmentation Course Program" —once only available directly and privately from the underground International Systemology Society.

Discover the amazing power behind the applied spiritual technology used for counseling and advisement in the Mardukite Zuism tradition.

SYSTEMOLOGY
The Pathway to Self-Honesty

METAHUMAN DESTINATIONS

*The Original 2020
Professional Piloting
Academy Course
for Grade IV*

by Joshua Free

*Mardukite Systemology
Liber-Two (2C,2D,3C)
Revised 2-Volume Set*

available individually

Drawing from the Arcane Tablets and nearly a year of additional research, experimentation and workshops since the introduction of applied spiritual technology and systematic processing methods, Joshua Free provides the ground-breaking manual for those seeking to correct—or "defragment"—the conditions that have trapped viewpoints of the Spirit into programming and encoding of the Human Condition.

Experience the revolutionary professional course in advanced spiritual technology for Mardukite Systemologists to "Pilot" the way to higher ideals that can free us from the Human Condition and return ultimate command and control of creation to the Spirit.

SYSTEMOLOGY
The Gateways to Infinity

IMAGINOMICON

Accessing the Gateway to Higher Universes

A New Grimoire for the Human Spirit

by Joshua Free

Mardukite Systemology Grade-IV Metahumanism, Wizard Level-0, Liber-3D

revised edition

The Way Out. Hidden for 6,000 Years.
But now we've found the Key.
A grimore to summon and invoke, command and control,
the most powerful spirit to ever exist.
Your Self.

Access beyond physical existence.
Fly free across all Gateways.
Go back to where it all began and reclaim that
personal universe which the *Spirit* once called "*Home.*"

Break free from the Matrix;
control the Mind and command the Body
from outside those systems
— because *You* were never "human" —
fully realize what it means to be a *spiritual being*,
then rise up through the Gateways to Higher Universes
and *BE.*

SYSTEMOLOGY
The Gateways to Infinity

SYSTEMOLOGY-180
The Fast-Track to Ascension

A Handbook for Pilots

by Joshua Free

*Mardukite Grade-V
Systemology
Liber-180*

*Expert application of
all Grade-III and Grade-IV
training and techniques*

A perfected "metahuman" state for the Human Condition awaits; free of emotional turbulence, societal programming and an ability to be truly Self-Determined from the clear perspective of the actual Self, the Eternal Spirit or "I-AM" Awareness that is back of and beyond this existence—an "Angel" or "god" that has fallen only by its own considerations, by being convinced that it resides locally here on earth within a perishable human shell.

"*Systemology-180*" presents newly revised instruction from the Mardukite Academy to deliver the fastest results in climbing the Ladder of Ascension. Hundreds of exercises and techniques that progressively free you from bonds of the Human Condition and increase your spiritual horsepower enough to break the chains and attachments to the material world and an existence confined to a material body.

SYSTEMOLOGY
The Gateways to Infinity

SYSTEMOLOGY:
BACKTRACK
**Reclaiming
Spiritual Power &
Past-Life Memory**

by Joshua Free

*Mardukite Grade-V
Systemology
Liber-4*

*Transcripts of the
original lectures
with diagrams
and glossary*

We are all Spiritual Beings that have known a very long
existence. Even before the evolution of Humans or Earth,
we existed as other forms, in other times and spaces.
We have descended down a very long *track* of potential
Beingness and considerations, a *track* that parallels the
allegory of "Fallen Angels" enticed by mundane bodies;
only to be trapped in them and longing to *Ascend* again.

*What if we could recover the long forgotten Knowingness of our
past existences? What if we could reclaim our true Spiritual power
that we have lost sight of? What if we could actually Backtrack
our descent and return to the Source?*

"*Backtrack*" documents the first advanced course given by
Joshua Free to the Systemology Society for Grade-V.
He candidly introduces the new Wizard-Level subject of
Alpha-Defragmentation to Grade-III and Grade-IV alumni
ready to embark on their next phase of the *Pathway*.

IN A WORLD FULL OF "TENS" BE AN
ELEVEN

THE METAPHYSICS OF STRANGER THINGS

TELEKINESIS, TELEPATHY SYSTEMOLOGY

by Joshua Free

Mardukite Systemology Liber-011

Experimental exploratory edition

Discover the metaphysical truth about the Universe—and maybe even yourself—as we explore what lies beneath the epic saga, *Stranger Things.* You're invited to a world where fantasy, science fiction and horror unite, and games like *Dungeons and Dragons* become reality.

Uncover a world of secret "mind control" projects, just like those at *Hawkins National Laboratory.* Decades of psychedelic experiments among other developmental programs for psychic powers, remote viewing, telekinesis (psychokinesis, PK) and more are revealed. Get an inside look at the operations of a real-life underground organization pursuing the truth about rehabilitating spiritual abilities for an actual "metahuman" evolution on planet Earth.

Premiere edition available in paperback and hardcover!

Commemorating the Mardukite 15th Anniversary!

NECRONOMICON
THE COMPLETE ANUNNAKI BIBLE
(*Deluxe Edition Hardcover Anthology*)
collected works by Joshua Free

The ultimate masterpiece of Mesopotamian magic, spirituality and history, providing a complete collection—a grand symphony—of the most ancient writings on the planet. The oldest Sumerian and Babylonian records reveal detailed accounts of cosmic history in the Universe and on Earth, the development of human civilization and descriptions of world order. All of this information has been used, since ancient times, to maintain spiritual and physical control of humanity and its systems. It has proved to be the predecessor and foundation of all global scripture-based religious and mystical traditions thereafter. These are the raw materials, unearthed from the underground, which have shaped humanity's beliefs, traditions and existence for thousands of years—right from the heart of the Ancient Near East: Sumer, Babylon and even Egypt...

The Original Classic Underground Bestseller Returns!
10th Anniversary Hardcover Collector's Edition.

SUMERIAN RELIGION

Introducing the Anunnaki Gods
of Mesopotamian Neopaganism

Mardukite Research Volume Liber-50

by Joshua Free

Develop a personal relationship with Anunnaki Gods
—the divine pantheon that launched a thousand
cultures and traditions throughout the world!

Even if you think you already know all about the Sumerian Anunnaki or Star-Gates of Babylon... ✳ Here you will find a beautifully crafted journey that is unlike anything Humans have had the opportunity to experience for thousands of years... ✳ Here you will find a truly remarkable tome demonstrating a fresh new approach to modern Mesopotamian Neopaganism and spirituality... ✳ Here is a Master Key to the ancient mystic arts: true knowledge concerning the powers and entities that these arts are dedicated to... ✳ A working relationship with these powers directly... ✳ And the wisdom to exist "alongside" the gods, so as to ever remain in the "favor" of Cosmic Law.

Also available in paperback as "*Anunnaki Gods*" by Joshua Free.

"*Babylonian Myth & Magic*" (*Liber-51+E*) sequel now available!

PUBLISHED BY THE **JOSHUA FREE** IMPRINT REPRESENTING

**The Founding Church of Mardukite Zuism
& Mardukite Academy of Systemology**

mardukite.com